To my family

olive oil sense and sensibility was made possible thanks to the collaboration of:

Photos: Walter and Laura Leonardi

Art director: Pino Brescia

Stylist: Giuseppe Armenise

Chef: Masseria San Domenico's chef

Technical Assistance: Alfredo Marasciulo

Translations: Richard Udal

Location: Masseria Cimino - Savelletri, Fasano

Special thanks for the courtesy of their photos: *Frantoio Raguso, pp. 46-47, 51*
Fig and Olives - NYC, p. 67
Gabriella Romano Modoni, p. 107
Gabrielino - Mattinata, p. 157

www.congedoeditore.it

ISBN 9788880868149

Colour processing and prepress: Fotolito38 - Bari
Printed: SEDIT – Bari

Rossella Speranza

olive oil sense and sensibility

Congedo Editore

Contents

Foreword .... p. 6
Introduction .... p. 8
The masseria .... p. 12
The olive tree .... p. 22
The harvest .... p. 34
The milling .... p. 42
The extra virgin olive oil .... p. 48
On the shelves .... p. 54
Storing .... p. 58
Tastings .... p. 62
At the table .... p. 66
Extra virgin olive oil with .... p. 70
... with bread .... p. 72
... with dairy products .... p. 82
... with cereals .... p. 90
... with fruits .... p. 98
... with meat .... p. 106
... with fish .... p. 112
... with pasta .... p. 120
... with vegetables .... p. 130
... with legumes .... p. 140
... in frying .... p. 148
... in desserts .... p. 156
... in cocktails .... p. 163
Vegetable preserves in oil .... p. 164
Aromatic olive oils .... p. 170
Olive oil and beauty .... p. 172
More... .... p. 178
FAQ Frequently Asked Questions .... p. 180
The Mediterranean Diet .... p. 182
Profile of the author .... p. 190
Acknowledgements .... p. 191
Sources .... p. 192

Foreword

When I first met Rossella Speranza, more than ten years ago, we began talking about olive oil. That conversation, I sometimes think, has never ceased since, as she has introduced me to so many ideas and personalities that count greatly in the world of olive oil. That world is full of passionate people but few can match Rossella's enthusiasm for this beloved product of her native soil. Now, with this book, she has focused her consuming interest and brought a story to the rest of us that, like its subject matter, is compelling and exciting and elegant all at the same time.

In many regards, the history of the Mediterranean is the history of olive oil. It is the foundation of both cuisine and agriculture, and the fundamental reason why nutrition scientists tell us that the Mediterranean diet is a good one. With olive oil (and one must assume we are speaking only of extra-virgin olive oil) we reach a kind of dietary apotheosis, balancing the goodness of fresh vegetables and seafood with a fat that isn't just "not bad" for us but downright beneficial, a monounsaturated fat that raises good cholesterol, lowers bad cholesterol, and brings with it loads of antioxidants and other valuable and little understood phytochemicals to promote good health.

But olive oil is so much more than that: It is indeed the very symbol of the Mediterranean, even when it comes from olives grown in California or New Zealand or South Africa. Olive trees, young and silvery leaved or ancient, twisted and gnarled, lend great beauty to the landscape as anyone knows who has seen the centenarian and even millenarian trees of Rossella's own Puglia. Just so, olive oil lends great beauty to the table, turning plain vegetables into elegant repasts, bathing humble crusts of garlic-rubbed bread with lush importance. Rossella helps us to focus on this miracle product which may well be the only super-food we know apart from mother's milk. And like mother's milk, olive oil takes us back to our own beginnings, back to the beginnings of our Western culture, and, if we're lucky, at the same time, sends us into the future full of good health and great food. Rossella Speranza's book, Olive Oil: Sense and Sensibility helps us find the way.

Nancy Harmon Jenkins

Food Journalist and Mediterranean cookbook author

Introduction

I was born in the south of Italy.

In the 1960s my family lived in Rome, but, for sentimental reasons, they chose my birthplace as my maternal grandparents' house, a villa surrounded by olive and almond trees in Puglia. In those days it wasn't easy to reach this region from the capital: the car journey took more than eight hours because the highway finished at Naples after which you had to drive through the Apennines, full of bends and hills.
It was a journey that we undertook twice a year, at Christmas and during the summer break, which we used to call "villeggiatura". The journey was never ending and when we finally reached the house in the country the reward was to be with our grandparents, our aunts and uncles, our cousins. We children immediately felt that we were under a magic spell.

I still think that the people from the south have a different conception of time and space which today we would define as "surreal", especially when referred to a rural context; during my childhood the difference between the countryside and the big cities was enormous. I can sincerely say that the thing that most struck me as a child was that in the south History stands still, that History that in the capital proceeded at such a great pace through fashion, automobiles, trends, protests ... in the south was proceeding at a slower pace...or there was simply no trace of it.

Clearly my baggage of memories has to include the tastes and smells that started from the morning with a breakfast of fresh fruit and continued, marking the summer day with its rhythms: milk fresh from the cow that was brought directly to the house, the smell of the wood-burning oven, the ritual of making the tomato sauce at the end of August.

The southern cuisine, the traditional one, is simple and unsophisticated and today its easy to understand why: the flavor of the ingredients, from the olive oil to the vegetables, the tomatoes, the bread and wine, have a strong flavor because they come from a land where the soil, the sun and the lack of water all contribute to concentrate the flavors

One of the flavors that I remember most clearly is that of the olive oil, that we call simply "oil". Bread with oil was our usual snack, the easiest thing to give us when we were hungry. Sometimes we would add a pinch of salt, some fresh tomato and oregano, but usually it was just a slice of bread and a "cross of oil".

This memory of an unmistakable taste is so clear that it has moved me, through the years, to investigate it further and has influenced my career choices. Extra-virgin olive oil can be metaphorically compared to a misunderstood child: it is a product of excellence, but without its due attention it risks becoming an "autism" favoring more accessible versions in terms of flavor and of price.
Yet olive oil speaks: the more you know it, the more you appreciate the subtleties of its character. And once you know it you'll never go back to lesser things.

I therefore felt the need to create a book that contains precise information from a technical point of view but has a narrative suitable for a reader who wants to know but doesn't want to study, also because it is the colors, the smells and the taste that give us the essence of food, in other words, our senses ...
In the first part I thought it best to follow two parallel routes: a physical journey around olive oil, from the fields to the table, since each phase contributes to the quality of the finished product, and a conceptual journey because if we don't know the characteristics of olive oil, we will never be able to make an aware choice.
The second part of the book is dedicated to a series of simple recipes that can be followed anywhere in the world, where the oil is mainly used uncooked, the best way to taste this condiment.

Of course, the text also contains some very personal opinions and suggestions that derive from 20 years of experience between Italy and the USA; olive oil owes much to the United States because it is American research over the last thirty years that has emphasized the importance of this food in our daily diet, with ever more important scientific evidence.

Olive oil, in its best form, that is extra-virgin, is the protagonist of this photographic book; in the background is the beauty of the places where it is produced, the light of the south, the magnificent olive trees and verses by those who have been inspired by its enchantment.

Rossella Speranza

You don't know the South,
the lime-washed houses
that we came out of into the sun
like numbers on the face of a dice.
Vittorio Bodini

... we live in an enchantment,
among buildings of tufa,
on a great plain.

Vittorio Bodini

The masseria

The masseria

One of the most characteristic rural settlements in southern Italy is the masseria, a fortified farmhouse that is very common in Puglia and Sicily, and which, just as with the *masias* in Spain and the *pousadas* in Portugal, is undergoing a happy phase of re-evaluation and restoration.

Today most masserias, both those used as a home and those used for tourism, are no longer working farms, but if we look carefully at their structure it is easy to recreate the organization for which they were conceived.

In the past the masseria was a territorial feature linked to the estate, that is the great areas of farmland that added to the income of the aristocratic and upper classes. The masserias were therefore great farms, sometimes inhabited by the landowners, but which included also the workers' lodgings, the stables, and the barns for storing forage and produce.

The birth of the masseria was often the result of the baronial colonization, in the sixteenth, seventeenth and eighteenth centuries, of vast inland areas that had been abandoned and left uncultivated, when Spain gave out licenses to re-populate the area to the noblemen of the Kingdom of the Two Sicilies in order to be supplied with cereals. These nobles even founded entire villages around the original construction.

A lot of the masserias were self-sufficient in the sense that all the procedures for transforming the agricultural produce were carried out within their walls; some were specialized in certain procedures, depending on the type of estate where they were situated.

Consequently, in the masserias near to pastures there was a lot of dairy

production, whereas those near olive and grape growing areas were equipped with mills for producing oil and presses for making wine.
The masseria used for the photographs in this book (Masseria Cimino) is in Puglia near the Valle d'Itria, just a few hundred yards from the Adriatic Sea. It is surrounded by centuries old olive groves, making the area unique in the world thanks to these natural monuments.
In the past the huge number of olive trees made it essential to produce the oil directly in these buildings, so many of the masserias have the remains of ancient oil mills within them. Naturally these are no longer in working order, but they make up an important historic artifact.
In the more southern part of Puglia, that is throughout the Salento, the mills tended to be "hypogea" that is subterranean. This is because it was easier to dig out the tufa rock than to build; tufa is in fact a very soft rock that was also used in the past for constructing villas and masserias.
The original stones from these mills, made up of two or three stone wheels that were pulled around inside special vats by pack animals, can still be seen. The pressing of the olives was then carried out in special presses where the olive paste was spread over the so-called "fiscoli", disks made of natural fiber.
As well as the mills within the individual masserias there were also many mills situated near the towns; throughout the olive season, which lasted several months, the mill workers lived underground, and their only means of communication with the outside world was via the hole through which the olives were delivered or through the narrow entrance: these mills were still in use until the end of the nineteenth century.
The world of the olive was cruel and dramatic, with men and beasts subjected to exhausting, but absolutely necessary work. At the end of a long process they obtained the olive oil, a precious product that was for centuries the basis of the economy of many Mediterranean regions.

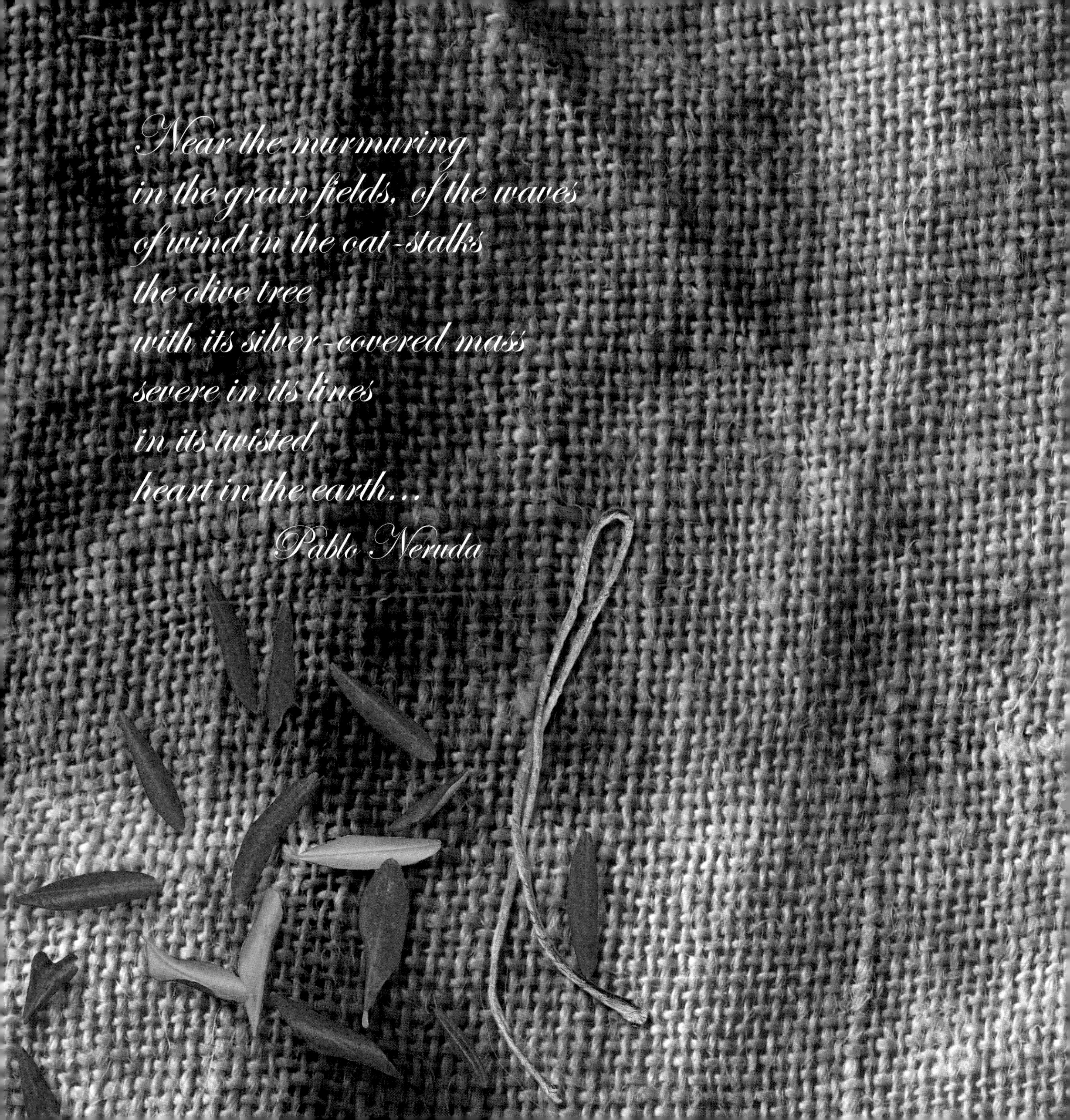

Near the murmuring
in the grain fields, of the waves
of wind in the oat-stalks
the olive tree
with its silver-covered mass
severe in its lines
in its twisted
heart in the earth...

Pablo Neruda

The olive tree

The olive tree

Looking at the Mediterranean region one cannot remain indifferent to the almost constant presence of the olive tree in all the countries that face onto this sea; closer inspection will reveal the extreme variations in the plant, so much so that some specimens don't seem to belong to the same species.
In the region covered by these photographs, for example, the monumental olive trees of the Salento area are very different from those of the central area of Puglia, which again are different from those on the Gargano peninsula. There are different varieties of plant, different ways of pruning and different ways of planting them on the land.
In the oldest olive groves the trees are planted in random order and are wide apart; the younger groves have the trees closer together and they are planted in rows: this is particularly clear when seen from above.
One characteristic always allows us to identify the olive, however: its silvery leaf, the unmistakable tint of the Mediterranean maquis.
The olive grows in lands where water is scarce. It has ancient origins and its use goes back to the beginning of man.
The olive tree was cultivated in Syria over 6,000 years ago. It seems that the Phoenicians were among the first peoples to cultivate it. In ancient times oil was used not only for cooking but also in the preparation of bread used in sacrifice, as well as a currency in trade, as a balm in medicine, in cosmetics and as a fuel for heating and lighting and to perfume the house. Its use was a cultural indication of the different societies.
Olive cultivation was very widespread among the Greeks and became systematic, in the sense that they began to establish the first rules for cultivating the trees, such as how to line

If somebody will have uprooted or pulled down an olive tree, either state or private owned, will be taken to Court and, in case of guilt, will be sentenced to death.

Aristotle
Constitution of Athenians

them up and the distance between them. It was the Greeks who introduced olive cultivation in all of Magna Grecia. The Romans, however, were the first to take the olive further north.
The Romans recognized many values in the oil, and in particular they appreciated its therapeutic qualities; they were the first to create tools for pressing the olives, and techniques for preserving the oil that remained almost unchanged until the nineteenth century.
Sacred and profane legends, religious and symbolic rites, mythological representations all added to the historic importance of olive cultivation and its great symbolic value. There are innumerable references to oil and the olive tree in Greek mythology and in the sacred texts of the three monotheistic religions.
Greek mythology tells us that there was once a dispute taken before the gods of Olympus between Athena and Poseidon for the land of Atticus. Zeus decided that he would give the land to the one who created the most useful thing: Poseidon created the horse, Athena simply planted an olive tree and taught its use and its cultivation. The victory was assigned to the latter and the Greek cult consecrated the olive tree to Athena.
In the Old Testament it is told that when the waters started to subside after the Great Flood, Noah sent a dove to fly out, it came back with an olive branch in its beak: from this Noah understood that the waters had withdrawn from the land. That is how the olive branch became the symbol of renewal and of peace between the Jews, the Christians and the Muslims.

In the Koran it is written that: "God is the light of the skies and of the land. His light is like that of the lamp, placed in a niche in a crystal bowl like a shining star, and lit thanks to a blessed tree, an olive that is neither in the east nor in the west, and whose oil would illuminate even if it were not touched by flame."

What has changed from ancient times to the present? Today the olive can be found on other continents, from North and South America to Australia, and this is thanks to the interest for olive oil in world markets.

It is, however, in the Mediterranean basin where 95% of global olive cultivation takes place, corresponding to roughly 800 million olive trees, or 8.5 million hectares.
Spain is the biggest producer of olive oil with about 35% of the total, followed by Italy with approximately 20%; Greece and the other Mediterranean producers follow. From these few statistics we can see that olive cultivation is an integral part of Mediterranean culture.
Olive trees have an incredibly long life, and reach maturity after about 20 years; from 35 to 150 years the plant produces the best olives. This means that the centuries old olive trees do not necessarily produce the best oil, but their monumental presence is of fundamental importance to the Mediterranean landscape: here the olive tree is a testimonial, life and enchantment.

In 2007 the regional government of Puglia in Italy passed the regional law to protect its centuries old olive trees. The law protects the five million monumental olive trees, valuable examples of the more than 60 million plants that mark the typical landscape of Puglia, many centuries old olive trees have been illegally uprooted in recent years, mainly to adorn villas and private gardens.
The law provides for ***promotional activities:*** *it allows for the denomination "extra-virgin olive oil from the centuries-old olive trees of Puglia" marking the product both ethically and in terms of quality, it also defines the way the landscape of olive groves can be promoted in terms of tourism and how farmers can be rewarded for action taken to preserve the monumental olive trees. The law also establishes the punishment for anyone who violates it.*

In ancient Greece, the gods were competing about whose
name should be given to the city that would shine
in civilization, culture and glory. Athena, the goddess
of wisdom, won by planting the olive tree, presaging
the discoveries that would put olive oil
at the epicenter of a health promoting diet.
Antonia Trichopoulou

... the graceful olives polished
by the hands which made the dove
and the oceanic snail:
green, innumerable,
immaculate nipples of nature ...

Pablo Neruda

The harvest

The harvest

What are the secrets of the harvest? What are the most important aspects for obtaining good quality oil? The first thing for a good harvest is that the fruit must be healthy, and this depends on using good cultivation techniques.

A well carried out harvest must have as its main objective the gathering of the fruit at the right degree of maturity and keeping it whole.

The degree of maturity depends on the type of cultivar, the latitude and altitude and the climatic conditions. In the Mediterranean the olive harvest is generally from mid-October (in the areas where they ripen earlier) to the end of January (where they ripen later).

Having said this, and bearing in mind that the olives should suffer as little damage as possible, it is clear that the way they are harvested will determine the state of the fruit: hand picking is the method that does the least damage to the fruit, but it is also the most costly system, as it uses a lot of labor. It is not always possible to pick by hand, however, especially when the tree is very large.

Today the most common techniques used are mechanically beating or shaking the trees, two methods that allow the fruit to be gathered in excellent condition.

Since the olives need to reach the press in as healthy a state as possible, the method of transport is also very important; they should be transported in low crates with plenty of air holes to stop the olives from rotting.

One should also know that ignoring certain rules before the pressing, and after for storing the oil will lead to damage to the finished product; experts can in fact tell, just by tasting, what exactly has caused a certain defect.

Delivery of the olives to the press must therefore be carried out as carefully and as quickly as possible. In general, the pressing should take place within 24 hours (maximum 48 hours) of the harvest.

Harvesting techniques

Hand picking directly from the plant. This is undoubtedly the method that does least damage to the fruit and allows it to be stored longer. In order to hand pick, various types of ladders are often used to reach the higher parts of the tree. For some time now various hand tools have been used instead of fingers, such as combs or small rakes, which make the process quicker and easier.

To increase productivity and substitute labor which is always harder to find, many farmers use **mechanical shakers**. Shaking the trunk and the branches of the tree causes the olives to fall into nets spread on the ground around the trees, or into large baskets. The end product is of a similar quality to that obtained through hand picking.

Beating is often used in groves where the trees are too big to allow hand picking. The olives are knocked down with sticks and fall into nets spread on the ground around the trees or into large baskets.

Finally there is the method of just letting the olives **drop,** a system used mainly in areas where the olive trees are too high for picking (around 5m). the olives are left to fall naturally when they are very ripe and are gathered with nets or from the ground.

The oil produced from olives gathered in this way are generally of very poor quality and not suitable for consumption.

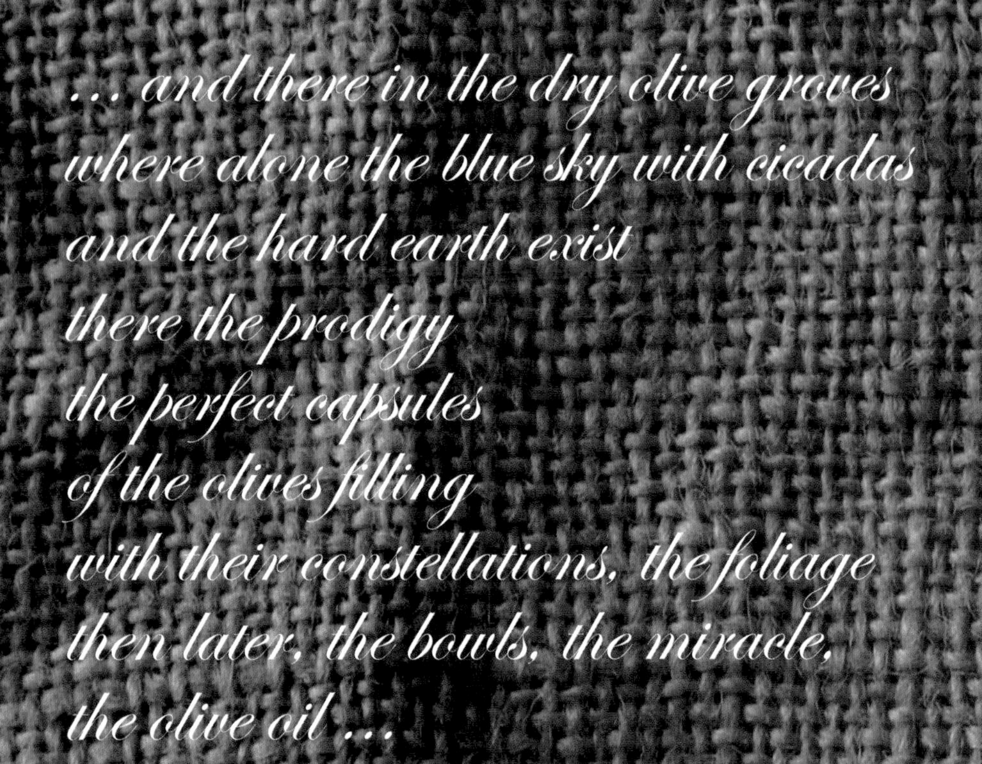

… and there in the dry olive groves
where alone the blue sky with cicadas
and the hard earth exist
there the prodigy
the perfect capsules
of the olives filling
with their constellations, the foliage
then later, the bowls, the miracle,
the olive oil …

Pablo Neruda

The milling

The milling

Extra virgin olive oil is the only vegetable fat obtained through the mechanical pressing of a fruit. All the other vegetable oils are obtained from the seeds and not the fruit (usually extracted chemically and not by pressing). This fact is very important for the characteristic naturalness of this product, and explains its long history if we consider that in ancient times man could extract oil mechanically but didn't know the techniques of chemical extraction. Nowadays there are two main methods of milling:

- the **traditional** method uses stone wheels (millstones), maybe a malaxer, and then pressing;
- the **continuous cycle** using a crusher (using hammers or star wheels), a malaxer and a horizontal or vertical centrifuge (or separator).

The phases for obtaining oil from the olives have not changed with respect to the past; in fact, despite the long history of olive oil, and continuous technological innovations the process for extracting the oil can be summarized in the three phases of crushing, malaxing and pressing (traditional) or extracting (modern).

From the crushing of the olives (breaking up the whole fruit made up of the pulp and the stones) they obtain a paste containing oil, water and solids (residues). This paste is malaxed to help the oil, saturating the paste, to come together; it is then pressed (extraction) which separates, depending on the process used, the two or three different components of the paste: the oil, the water (so called "from vegetation" and the solids (residue). Further operations such as decanting and maybe filtering produce the oil as we usually buy it.

Like the harvesting and the transportation, also the processing is a very delicate phase and the quality of the final product derives directly from the experience and professional approach of the press operator whose work can be compared to an art form.

There are more than 6,000 oil mills in Italy throughout the peninsula. The majority of them are in the South where nearly eighty percent of Italian oil production takes place.

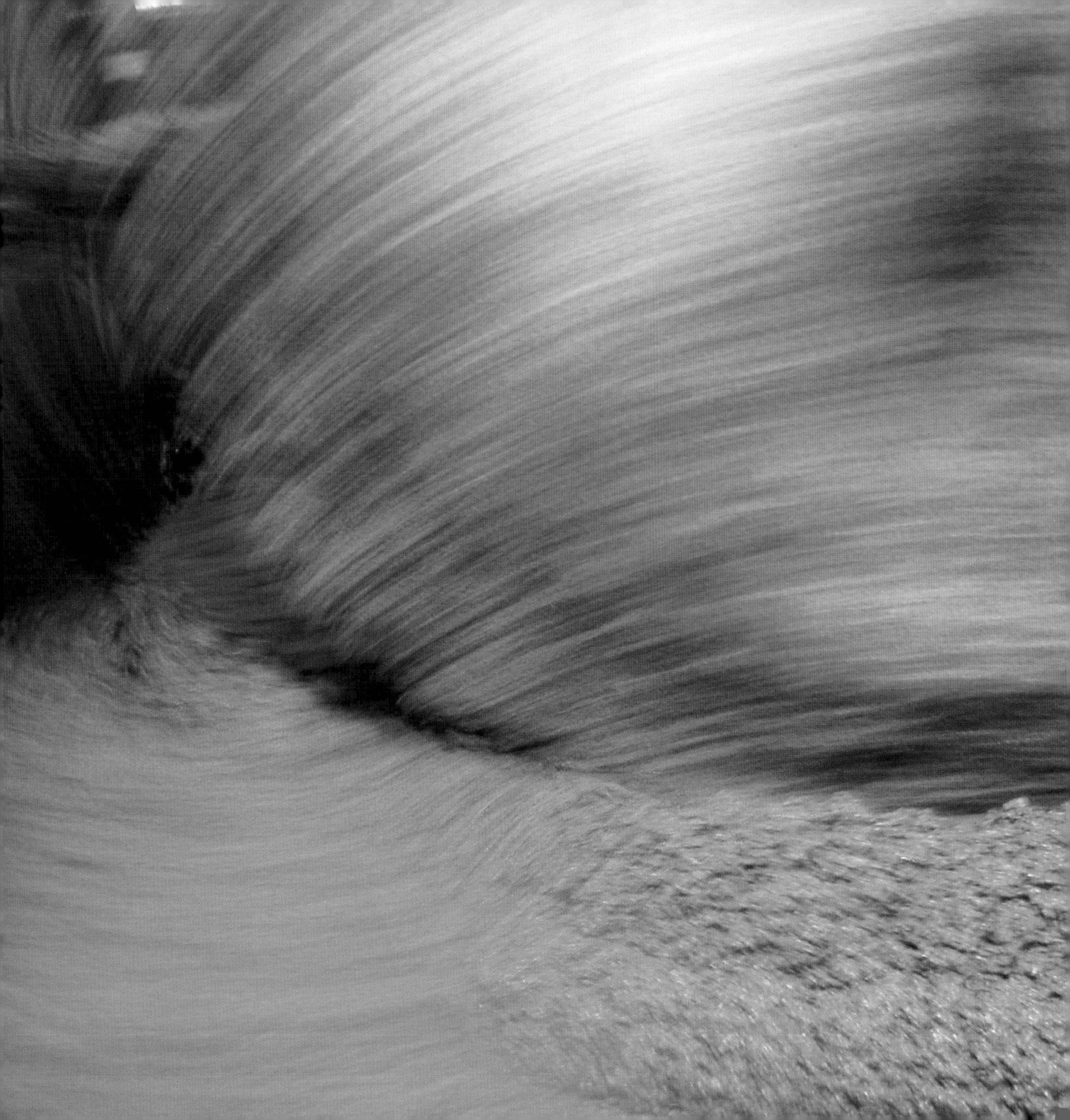

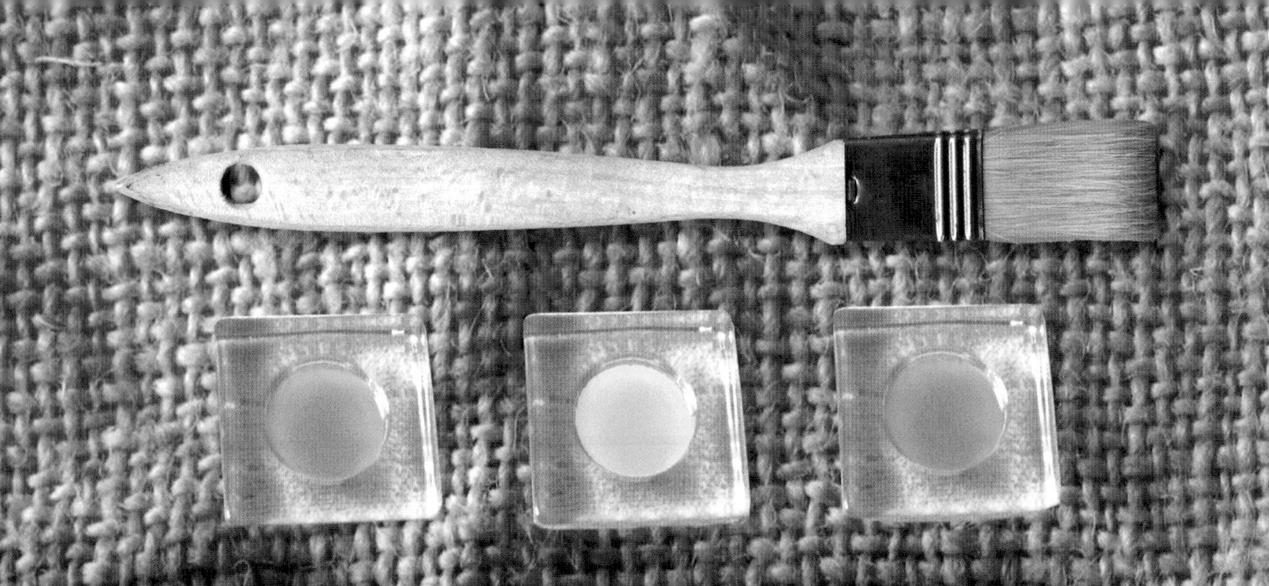

... I love the homelands of olive oil
the olive groves of Chacabuco, in Chile
in the morning feathers
of platinum forests of them
against the wrinkled mountain ranges.
In Anacapri, up above,
over the light of the Italian sea
is the despair of olive trees
and on the map of Europe Spain
a black basketful of olives
dusted off by orange blossoms
as if by a sea breeze ...

Pablo Neruda

The extra virgin olive oil

The extra virgin olive oil

There is a linguistic problem in the use of the term "olive oil": this can easily be understood in a land that boasts a thousand year culinary tradition and where we have always spoken about "oil" and "olive oil".
The title of this book deliberately uses this colloquial language because the whole world speaks of "olive oil" to differentiate it from "seed oil".
Things change, of course, when we get into the specifics and we have to choose an oil from the shelves. In fact there is a lot of confusion over olive oils. The ordinary consumer faced by oils with different labels (extra virgin olive oil, virgin olive oil, olive oil, pomace olive oil [*olio di sansa*]), while understanding the difference is not able to make an informed choice because he doesn't have sufficient knowledge of the rules that govern the sector, the production processes the chemical and sensory values that make up the basis of oil classification.

Since this book aims at simplifying an approach to oil it is important first of all to know that current European laws distinguish virgin olive oils from those that are not virgin:

- **virgin olive oils** are obtained by a simple pressing of the fruit
- **refined oils** are obtained through chemical processes

Oils from the presses are therefore virgin, but not necessarily extra virgin. To be extra virgin the oil must meet two essential parameters: one of them chemical, the other sensory. The chemical analysis is carried out in a laboratory, while the sensory one is carried out by a panel of 8-12 experts, members of a specific national professional body of Tasters of virgin olive oils.
To be extra virgin an olive oil must meet a series of parameters including not exceeding 0.8% acidity[1] (from chemical analysis) and there must be no sensory de-

fects (result of the sensory analysis).

What it is important to know is that when buying a bottle of oil labeled **"olive oil"** you are buying an oil that had defects that have been rectified by mixing it with a percentage (often tiny) of extra virgin oil. Therefore, in order to avoid misunderstandings, it is important to know if the denomination "olive oil" is used in a colloquial way meaning "extra virgin olive oil" or if it indicates a label, in this case it is not "extra virgin".

"Pomace olive oil is obtained from the "pomace", solid residue left from the pressing of the olives, and is produced in factories known as "santifici".

There is a classification of olive oils regulated by European Community rules[2].

Why is extra virgin olive oil the best of the edible oils?

Because it has significant amounts of antioxidants which are very important for our health and because, unlike other oils with a more bland flavor, it gives Mediterranean dishes, and not only, that special touch of flavor and freshness.
At this point I should specify that there is an objective criterion which is the basis of a good extra virgin olive oil and this, as has already been seen, is the result of laboratory analyses and sensory analyses, and a subjective criterion linked to the taste of the consumer.
The most important example of the difference that often exists between objective and subjective criteria when talking of oil is connected with the "peppery" taste of the extra virgin oil of some cultivars (such as the "coratina" variety): this stinging spiciness is not appreciated by the majority of consumers who mistakenly take it for a high level of acidity, and therefore see it as a defect (subjective criterion), yet the spiciness is caused by the presence of polyphenols that are powerful antioxidants (objective criterion).
Some producers get around this problem by mixing oils from different cultivars to obtain a more balanced taste, and we must recognize that

there is an increased level of professionalism in this sector. Despite this, it is of fundamental importance that the consumer is gradually helped to recognize the sensory characteristics of extra virgin olive oil and the differences between the flavors of the various cultivars; these differences are extremely important for a correct matching of different oils with various dishes.

We must not forget that in recent decades tastes have become much more bland, favoring neutral oils that are more like lubricants than condiments, which has not only had a negative effect on the dishes but also on the whole oil producing industry: there is a whole world linked to high quality olive cultivation that quite rightly wants a leading role in guiding the consumer, particularly the consumer who is sensitive to aspects of taste and health.

[1] The acidity refers to the percentage of free fatty acids and is a laboratory statistic and therefore not determined by tasting.

[2] The descriptions and definitions of olive oils and of pomace olive oils were established by EC Regulation 1531/2001 emitted by the Council on 23rd July 2001 and in force since 1st November 2003 E.E.C. Ruling n. 2568/91 Annex XII

A good extra virgin olive oil is at its best when it is fresh (there is a proverb that says *new oil, old wine*), but after 12-18 months it loses most of its flavor. The oil doesn't become toxic or dangerous, but it loses a lot of its components and changes bouquet and flavor.

There are, of course, cultivars that have more antioxidants, helping them to maintain their sensory qualities longer, but generally one should not buy an extra virgin oil that is more than one year old.

Since heat, oxygen and light cause a rapid oxidation, oil should always be conserved in a tightly closed container in a cool dark place. The containers should be full where possible to stop air from aiding the oxidation.

When we see extra virgin olive oil on the supermarket shelves we should choose:

- extra virgin olive oil with a clear indication of the producer (legal requirement);
- extra virgin olive oil packaged in dark bottles;
- extra virgin olive oil produced during the latest harvest.

The **date of harvest** can be calculated by looking at the "best by" date which is generally 18-24 months after the harvest.

There is a series of additional information that may be on the label; the most common is:

- the term **Organic ("*biologico*")** attributed to those products grown and processed without the use of herbicides or pesticides that disturb the equilibrium of nature. The law recognizes public and private bodies that check and certify the term organic;
- the **DOP** seal (Denominazione di

Origine Protetta) [PDO – Protected Designation of Origin] guarantees the place of origin of the extra virgin olive oil, the method of cultivation and production, and therefore the quality characteristics. Extra virgin olive oils are not all the same, they have different flavors and bouquets according to their region of origin. The PDO seal identifies the oil and guarantees the protection of both the typical characteristics to the consumer, since the seal is conferred only to extra virgin olive oils produced in full respect of the area of origin. European Union legislation of the PDO seal applies the so-called criterion of traceability that allows the consumer to know the real origin of the product he is buying.

The **concept of traceability** is today extremely important for the consumer and there is currently (2008) a significant political battle to have the origin of the olives clearly shown on the label and not just the place of pressing, for all types of olive oil.

It is, however, very important to know that a quality extra virgin oil can only be called such if it has been produced properly, that is if all the basic rules for making oil have been followed. The quality does not depend on the origin of the product.

The oil market can be separated into two distinct sectors: the first, and most important one in terms of quantity, is linked to the large bottling industry that is not involved in production but buys its oil from oil mills and cooperatives. The bottling industry is not involved in the production phases; it does however have the merit of having spread the culture of olive oil throughout the world and of having got the consumer used to this condiment in the importing countries.

The second type of market is that of the direct sales between the producer and/or the mill and the consumer.

VC
Extra Virgin Olive Oil
Private Label
Direct from the Grove
Product of Puglia, Italy
3 Liters
Olio extra vergine
di oliva
della Masseria San Domenico
Azienda Agricola San Domenico
Fasano (Brindisi)
Olio extra vergine
di oliva
della Masseria San Domenico
Azienda Agricola San Domenico
Fasano (Brindisi)

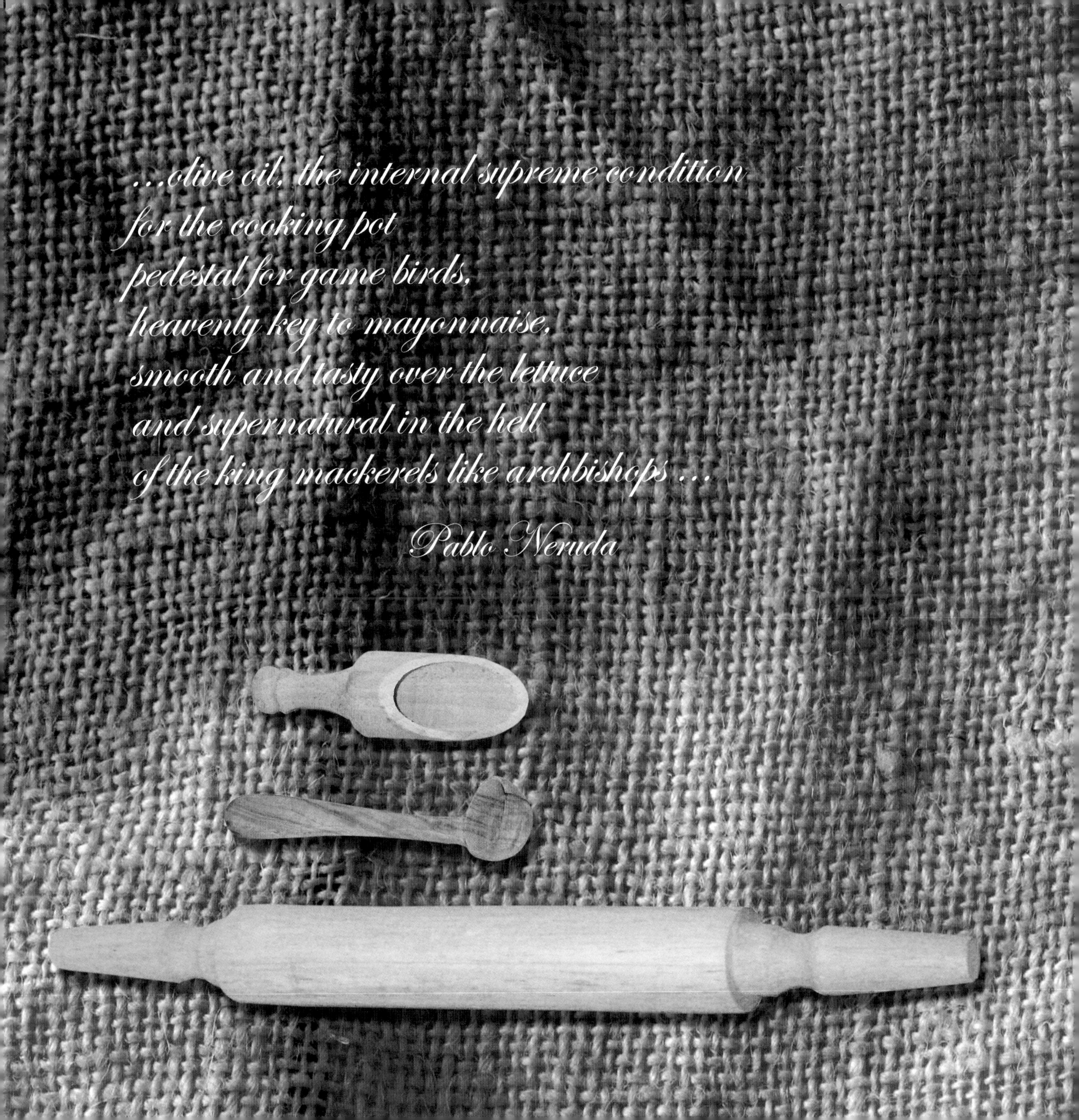

...olive oil, the internal supreme condition
for the cooking pot
pedestal for game birds,
heavenly key to mayonnaise,
smooth and tasty over the lettuce
and supernatural in the hell
of the king mackerels like archbishops ...

Pablo Neruda

Storing

Storing in the kitchen

Extra virgin olive oil needs to be kept away from light and in a cool place, since light and heat can damage the bouquet and the taste.

It should be stored in stainless steel containers, which are easy to wash with only water, will protect from the light and are much more hygienic than other containers. Small stainless steel cans can be found (3 and 5 liters) which are also decorative.

It is generally unwise to store oil in transparent bottles unless it is being used daily (which is advisable); however, bottles should be kept away from direct light and heat.

The life of extra virgin oil is relatively short, it shouldn't be kept more than a year, so before buying large quantities of oil you should keep this in mind.

Storing oil for longer than a year its color pales and the characteristic scent of the young oil gradually disappears.

In technical terms tasting is called **sensorial analysis;** it evaluates the characteristics of a food that interact with our organs of sense. The senses that are most involved in the perception of the sensory characteristics of food are taste, smell and sight.
It is important to remember that olive oil is the first food for which sensorial analysis, based on a system of panel-testing by a group of expert tasters, is used to distinguish different products, in other words the European Union (E.E.C. Ruling n. 2568/91 Annex XII) establishes that an oil must be subjected to tasting in order to determine, through a system of points, the category of commodity to which it belongs.
In the past the quality of olive oil was established purely on the basis of traditional chemical analysis to ascertain in particular its acidity. But the evaluation of only chemical parameters is not enough to guarantee that an oil has good sensorial qualities. It is possible, in fact that an oil with excellent chemical values has sensorial defects (taste, aroma, bouquet) that make it a poorer quality product.
A lot of the possible sensations perceived in tasting virgin oils are identified using official terminology established by European Union ruling.
Generally the sensorial analysis takes place using small blue glasses to stop the taster from being influenced by the color. There can, in fact, be an infinite range of shades of color, from bright green to deep gold, and this is not a good measure of the quality of the product.
After warming the glass in his hands,

...our chorus
with intimate powerful smoothness
you sing: you are the Spanish language
there are syllables of olive oil
there are words useful and rich-smelling
like your fragrant material ...
Pablo Neruda

the taster sniffs the bouquet before tasting. It is interesting to remember that as well as the pleasurable sensations that arise there can also be unpleasant sensations deriving from all the possible negligence during the harvest, the transport and the pressing. To that we must add the importance of correct storage both by the retailer and by the end consumer because these too make up the final condition of the extra virgin olive oil.

Virtues

Bitter: that taste, which is pleasurable at the right degree, that characterizes an oil made from olives pressed while still green;
Peppery: the tactile, burning sensation typical of oils produced at the beginning of the season, mainly from green olives;
Fruity: oil with a taste and perfume of fresh, healthy olives picked at the perfect point of ripeness. It is the only quality that can be perceived directly through smelling;
Grass: reminiscent of freshly cut grass;
Almondy: term associated with sweet oils with a delicate bouquet, the sensation is reminiscent of fresh or dried almonds. The latter is sometimes confused with a latent rancidness;
Apple: reminiscent of this fruit.

Defects

Rancid: unpleasant flavor that cannot be rectified, typical of oils that have oxidized through prolonged contact with the air;
Heating: typical taste of oils taken from olives that have been piled up and were over-ripe;
Vegetation water: the defect that an oil acquires when it has been decanted badly or has been left for a long period in contact with the water in the paste;
Fermented: when the oil has a taste of vinegar or wine because the olives have started to ferment producing more acetic acid , ethyl acetate and ethanol than normal;
Cooked: caused by excessive or lengthy heating of the oil during the extraction phase, especially when the malaxing phase is not carried out in the correct conditions;
"Fiscoli": when the oil extracted from the olive paste has been contaminated by fermented residue on dirty "fiscoli" disks;
Coarse: the oral-tactile feeling, dense and pasty, that some oils leave on tasting;
Metallic: the metallic flavor that derives from keeping the oil for a long time in incorrect conditions in contact with metal surfaces during the crushing, malaxing, pressing or when the olives have been left piled together;
Sludge: the sensation of oil that has been extracted from the decantation sediment or that has been too long in contact with its own sediment, resulting in anaerobic fermentation;
Mold: the sensation of those oils that have been extracted from fruit that has been piled up for several days in a damp place with fungi and yeasts starting to grow;
Earth: when the olives are gathered from the ground, particularly when they are not washed, the olives take on this flavor.

At the table, discretion and imagination rule.
Meals are a convivial moment when the host can freely decide whether to serve the extra virgin oil in the dark bottles in which, presumably, it was packed or in transparent oil cruets where you can see the color and the aspect or in special bowls.
Naturally the host, especially if there are various different oils at the table, will explain their origin, their characteristics etc.
Fortunately extra virgin olive oil has started to have an important role in top quality restaurants. In this context the current trend is to give added value to the oil through information (eg. oil lists) and training (advice by the chefs).
There are some very innovative examples of marketing olive oil at the table aimed also at a very young audience, surprising them with a fun approach.
One of the most significant examples is the *Fig & Olive* in New York, a Mediterranean inspired restaurant that has made extra virgin olive oil the symbol of its cuisine.

… it's not only wine that sings olive oil sings too
it lives in us with its ripe light
and among the good things of the earth
I set apart olive oil, your ever-flowing peace, your green essence
your heaped-up treasure which descends
in streams from the olive tree.
Pablo Neruda

The true cook must be mature; she must know the world from her social point of view, however humble it be; she must have pondered concerning good and evil, in however lowly and incongruous a fashion; ...

Norman Douglas

Recipes
Extra virgin
olive oil with...

"Bread and oil" is the classic combination, perhaps the best way to taste extra virgin oil and not only; it is one of the healthiest snacks as long as the bread is good as well as the oil!
The tradition of bread is so rich that it deserves some special attention. There is a rule of the Medical School of Salerno (VIII-XIX centuries) on the necessary qualities of the bread to be served at table: not too hot, nor too old, from selected wheat, well leavened, slightly salted and well cooked.
In the following recipes we have used home made bread made with selected wheat (durum wheat and soft wheat), naturally leavened (the so called mother leavening) and cooked in a wood burning oven. This type of bread is the most suitable for "bruschetta" (toasted bread) and for all the traditional dishes, some of which use stale bread.
The use of stale bread goes back to the peasant culture and, although it clearly derives from a need to save, it is a very healthy and tasty custom. In fact, as bread ages it goes through a series of changes (for example the retrogradation of the starch) that make it easier to digest. Naturally leavened bread (known also as sour dough) goes stale slower than that leavened with brewers yeast. This is why in old times, the bread, which was often home made, lasted almost a week.
An excellent substitute for stale bread is the so-called "frisella", a donut shaped biscuit made of durum wheat (or barley) cooked in a wood-burning oven, it is broken horizontally in half and toasted; before eating, it should be softened with water.

CAPUT XXIV. DE PANE
Panis non calidus, nec sit nimis inveteratus,
sed fermentatus, oculatus sit, bene coctus,
modice salitus: frugibus validis sit electus.
Non comedas crustam, choleram quia gignit adustam.
Panis salsatus, fermentatus, bene coctus,
purus sit, sanus, quia non ita sit tibi vanus.
Bread not hot, nor old,
Well leavened, visibly well cooked,
Slightly salted: selected from good quality wheat.
Avoid eating the crust, because the burnt parts are bad for you,
It should be tasty, leavened, well cooked,
It should be pure, healthy, if not it will bring no benefit.
Regimen Sanitatis Salernitanum,

In order to simplify the pairing extra virgin olive oil has been classified in:

delicate fruity, medium fruity, insensely fruity

Bruschetta

Bruschetta is a poor man's dish from Italian peasant culture that is today generally eaten as a starter.
Traditional bruschetta is prepared with home-made bread, fresh or stale, that is toasted; rub some garlic over the surface and dress it with extra virgin olive oil.
Today there are many variations of bruschetta, the most common of these is with fresh tomato and arugula, but the original is with oil and garlic.

Suggestion: intensely fruity extra virgin oil

Gazpacho

Gazpacho is a cold soup originally from Andalusia made of raw vegetables. It was a peasant dish that used to be carried to the fields in wine skins, it was eaten at the workplace in its semi-liquid form and is refreshing and tasty. There are at least 60 versions, some of them very spicy, often with varying quantities of paprika added.

Ingredients

- 28 ounces Red tomatoes
- 1 cucumber
- 3 1/2 ounces stale bread
- 1 red onion
- 1 clove of garlic
- Pepper (to taste)
- 1 cup extra virgin olive oil
- White wine vinegar (to taste)
- Salt (to taste)
- Water (to taste)

Preparation

First blend the ingredients, tomatoes, peppers, cucumbers, onion, and then strain it, removing all the seeds and pieces of peel left in the mixture. Add the garlic, bread, oil and a little vinegar and salt. Add water to give the gazpacho the consistency required, either as a light cream or thicker. After blending everything once more, place it in the fridge to settle.
Serve cold in a cup or glass, you can even put ice cubes in it and serve with croûtons and diced vegetables.

Suggestion: medium fruity extra virgin olive oil

Pancotto

Pancotto is a traditional Italian peasant dish which derives from home economics where the stale bread was used.
There are so many varieties of pancotto, not only because this is a traditional regional dish, but also because the vegetables available change according to the season.
In fact, for this dish you can use chard, chicory, rocket, broccoli rabe, or mixed wild herbs. In some cases zucchini and potatoes are used.

Ingredients

- 4 1/2 pounds broccoli rabe
- 8 slices of stale home made bread
- 3 cloves of garlic
- Salt (to taste)

Preparation

Clean the broccoli rabe and boil them in salted water with the garlic. Put the slices of bread in a colander and drain part of the vegetables on to them. The boiling water will soften the bread. Pour the rest of the broccoli rabe into a soup tureen and add the already drained ones with the bread. Serve hot and dress with extra virgin olive oil.

Suggestion: medium or intensely fruity extra virgin olive oil

Panzanella

Panzanella is a very simple dish based on stale bread.

Ingredients

- Stale bread
- Diced raw tomato
- Red onion
- Basil or oregano
- Extra virgin olive oil
- Wine vinegar
- Salt

Preparation

In Tuscany the bread is left to soak in water and then squeezed until it crumbles. It is then mixed into the other ingredients.
The same dish in Puglia is called *cialledda* and in this region, instead of stale bread, we often use a frisella. This is softened in water before being crumbled.
The dish should be eaten at room temperature.

Suggestion: medium or intensely fruity extra virgin olive oil

...with dairy products

In Mediterranean cuisine there are many dishes that use fresh dairy products: just think of feta cheese in Greek salad, the widespread use of yogurt in Greece and Turkey and the use of mozzarella and ricotta in Italy.
Fresh cheeses and yogurt are by nature very versatile and, thanks to their low calorie content compared to seasoned cheeses, are often recommended for diets.
The combination of olive oil and dairy products is not traditional but in recent years, thanks to the improving quality of both of these products, it has become a winner because it exalts the taste of both the oil and the cheese, which should preferably be fresh.
Extra virgin olive oil, therefore, goes well with mozzarella, with robiola and with tomini.
The best combination, however, is with fresh goat's cheese which, by no coincidence, is also used in mixed salads.

Caprese salad

Caprese is a typical Mediterranean dish, so called because it was apparently "invented" by a restaurateur on the island of Capri. In a caprese you can really taste the basic ingredients, that is tomato, fresh mozzarella, and extra virgin olive oil, to which you just add salt and some fresh basil leaves. The best version of this salad needs so-called "sorrentine tomatoes" - large pinkish tomatoes that grow near Sorrento. These are sliced and placed with alternate layers of fiordilatte or buffalo mozzarella. This is then dressed with salt, oil and basil. The mozzarella must, of course, be very fresh, preferably of the day.
It is said that the English writer Norman Douglas, who chose the island of Capri as his *buen retiro*, would personally go to the restaurants in the morning to inspect the ingredients of the day to check that the fish was just caught and the mozzarella were "dripping, dripping with freshness".

Ingredients

- 1 pound of cherry tomatoes
- 1 pound of small round mozzarellas
- Extra virgin olive oil
- 10 leaves of fresh basil
- Salt to taste

Preparation

Place the washed tomatoes in a serving dish together with the round mozzarellas to form a small mound. Dress with salt, extra virgin olive oil and whole fresh basil leaves.

Suggestion: medium fruity extra virgin olive oil

Fresh caprino cheese

Ingredients

- 6 fresh caprino cheeses
- Ground black pepper
- Sweet paprika powder
- Extra virgin olive oil

Preparation

Pour the extra virgin olive oil onto the bottom of a dish and place the fresh caprino cheeses on it. Dust them alternately with the ground black pepper and the sweet paprika. Serve with fresh bread or croûtons.

Tzatziki

Tzatziki is a very popular Greek sauce made of yogurt and cucumbers; the traditional version is prepared with sheep or goat's yogurt. This sauce can be eaten on its own or with meat dishes.

Ingredients

- 1 pound Greek yogurt
- 4-5 cloves of garlic
- 1 cucumber
- 2 spoonfuls of white wine vinegar
- 4 spoonfuls of extra virgin olive oil
- Salt (to taste)

Preparation

Grate the cucumber without peeling it. Place it in a drainer, salt it and leave it for about an hour to drain some of its water. Peel the garlic and crush it. In a dish mix the drained cucumber, the yogurt, the crushed garlic, the vinegar, the salt and the olive oil. You can conserve this sauce in the fridge.

Suggestion: delicately fruity extra virgin olive oil

Extra virgin olive oil with cereals, as well as being an excellent mix, allows the creation of simple, light dishes that use raw oil and can be kept in the fridge for a few days.

The most suitable cereals for cooking and dressing with raw extra virgin olive oil are wheat, barley, spelled and of course, rice. Oats, which are usually sold as flakes, deserve separate mention.

Wheat is the cereal most widely eaten by Europeans; there is hard wheat and soft wheat and it is also sold as whole grains. As with all cereals, it takes a lot of cooking which is why it is best to soak it over night with a little bicarbonate. Nowadays, just like rice, you can find it *parboiled* which takes just ten minutes to cook.

Spelled is a very old cereal that was the basic food of the Romans for centuries. Spelled can be bought in two ways: dehulled spelled (or just spelled) and pearl spelled. Dehulled spelled is of course easier to digest because it contains more fiber, while the pearled version, which has had the outer layer removed, is whiter and cooks much more quickly.

Barley is different from the other cereals because of its high fiber content and together with oats it has the lowest glycemic content. There are two types of barley on sale: once again dehulled barley, which takes longer to cook and should be soaked before, and pearl barley which has been refined and therefore needs less cooking time.

The most widely used cereal in the world is, of course, **rice,** the basic foodstuff of billions of people, and this too is excellent with raw extra virgin olive oil.

It is very important to remember that all cereals are particularly good for you if eaten in the whole grain form. So whole **wheat, brown rice, spelled and dehulled barley, whole wheat pasta and bread** are not only very tasty but also are beneficial to health.

Wheat salad

Grains of cereals like durum wheat, spelled or barley can be the basis of very simple dishes like salads that, as well as being very light, can be kept in the fridge for several days.
These cereals generally need to be soaked beforehand, but ready cooked grains can be found that allow a faster preparation.
These salads can be prepared with many different types of raw fresh vegetables, but in this version vegetables preserved in extra virgin olive oil were used.

Ingredients

- 10 ounces wheat (also pre-cooked)
- 9 ounces dried tomatoes in extra virgin oil
- 9 ounces artichokes in extra virgin oil
- 9 ounces zucchini in extra virgin oil
- 9 ounces mushrooms in extra virgin oil

Preparation

Boil the wheat in a large quantity of salted water, drain it and leave it to cool.

Add the vegetable preserves, diced. Keep in the fridge.

Suggestion: medium fruity extra virgin olive oil

Rice salad

Rice salad is a very versatile summer dish that can be prepared with either white or brown rice. If you choose white rice it is better to use the variety where the grains remain whole. The vegetables used should always be in season.

Ingredients

- 10 ounces rice
- 3 salad tomatoes
- 1 stick of celery
- 1 cucumber
- 2 carrots
- 1 ounce capers
- Black olives
- Salt
- Extra virgin olive oil

Preparation

Cook the rice in a large quantity of salted water. After draining add the diced vegetables and dress with salt and extra virgin olive oil.

Suggestion: medium fruity extra virgin olive oil

Oat soup

Oats are generally sold as flakes. In the USA these have always been used a lot at breakfast with fresh fruit or in the sweet version (oat meal).
Here oat flakes are used in a way that the Americans will find unusual but very pleasant if you like simple healthy dishes that don't take much preparation.
Oat soup is an almost instant dish, an excellent semolina substitute and as such also suitable for children.

Ingredients

- 3 ounces of oat flakes
- 2.5 cups of water
- Salt to taste
- Parmesan cheese to taste
- Extra virgin olive oil

Preparation

Bring the slightly salted water to boil and add the oat flakes.
Leave it to cook for two minutes stirring frequently.
Serve with a cross of oil and grated Parmesan cheese.

Suggestion: delicate or medium fruity extra virgin olive oil

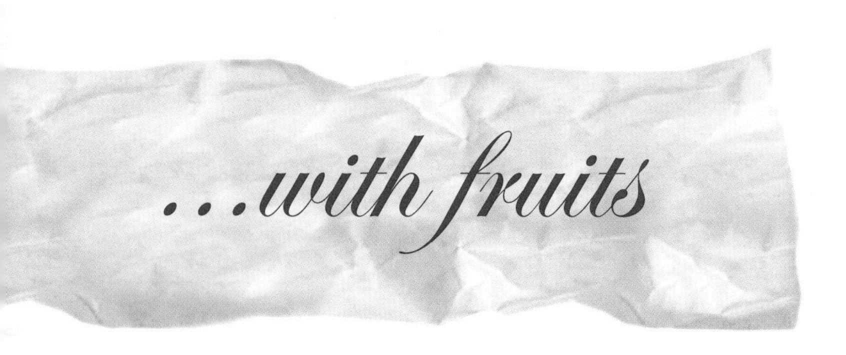

The combination of olive oil and fruit seems unusual, but some of the recipes have their roots in the the peasant tradition of some regions of the South.

One of the examples of a traditional recipe is the typical Sicilian fresh orange salad from the citrus growing areas. In the Mineo plain, near Catania, the peasant farmers used to prepare this salad during the orange harvest, dressing it with just oil and salt.

Of course for oil to go well with fruit the fruit must have the right degree of ripeness, but in any case not too ripe. It is therefore preferable to use oranges, apples or pears that are crisp and slightly bitter.

There are infinite variations on the oil-fruit theme because they can be combined with various salads (lettuce and green salad), florentine fennel, spring onions, white or black olives and, in some cases, herrings or anchovies. Dried fruit can also be added, such as walnuts, almonds, pine nuts.

Extra virgin olive oil, preferably lightly or medium fruited, sometimes with traditional balsamic vinegar, is the perfect complement to these.

Orange salad

Traditional orange salad is prepared by simply slicing oranges, preferably blood oranges, after having carefully removed the peel and the pith. These are then placed on a plate and dressed with extra virgin olive oil, salt and white wine vinegar.
A more complete version (see photo) has oranges with lettuce (green lettuce or romanella). In this case the oranges are chopped into small pieces in order to mix them better with the lettuce. It is then dressed with extra virgin olive oil, salt, white wine vinegar or balsamic vinegar.

Ingredients

- 4 seedless oranges
- 2 romanella lettuces
- Extra virgin olive oil to taste
- Balsamic vinegar to taste
- Salt to taste
- Orange peel

Preparation

After carefully washing the lettuce cut it into medium sized leaves; clean the oranges and place the round slices of 2 of the 4 oranges in the center of the dish. Place the lettuce on top of the oranges. Remove the peel from the remaining oranges, cut them into small pieces and place them on top of the lettuce. Dress with salt, oil and a little balsamic vinegar. Garnish with very thin slices of orange peel.

Suggestion: delicately fruity extra virgin olive oil

Apple, arugula and walnut salad

Another way to prepare salads with fruit is to add nuts. Walnuts, almonds, pine nuts and pistachios are ideal and are nutritionally complementary.
The salad prepared here uses Granny Smith apples which are probably the most suitable for salads as they are crisp and slightly sour. The apples were diced with the peel and mixed with the arugula and the walnuts, and then dressed with extra virgin olive oil and salt.
This is also excellent with the addition of traditional balsamic vinegar.

Ingredients

- 4 Granny Smith apples
- 2 handfuls of arugula
- 8 walnut kernels
- Extra virgin olive oil to taste
- Salt to taste
- Balsamic vinegar to taste

Preparation

Carefully wash the apples and cut them into cubes without peeling them. Carefully wash the arugula and cut the leaves in half. Add the roughly crumbled walnut kernels. Mix the ingredients and add salt, oil and a little balsamic vinegar.

Suggestion: delicately fruity extra virgin olive oil

Pear and pecorino cheese salad

The combination of fruit and cheese is not unusual in the Italian tradition, particularly pears and cheese. In fact, combining the two highlights the flavor of each.
This happy combination can be rounded off with the addition of green salad, arugula or romanella, and of course extra virgin olive oil. The most suitable pears are the Williams or Kaiser varieties, while the pecorino should be medium aged. I advise adding traditional balsamic vinegar.

Ingredients

- 4 Williams or Kaiser pears
- 2 romanella lettuces
- 7 ounces of semi-seasoned pecorino cheese
- Extra virgin olive oil to taste

Preparation

Carefully wash the lettuce and place a small bed of it on the dish.
Carefully wash the pears and thinly slice them lengthwise. Lay the sliced pears on the lettuce. Cut the pecorino cheese into flakes and place them on the sliced pears. Dress with extra virgin olive oil.

Suggestion: delicately fruity extra virgin olive oil

Meat, and in particular red meat, is not very common in Mediterranean cuisine.
However, traditional Mediterranean cuisine is not vegetarian; it's just that the meat used in traditional dishes is not beef: in Greece they eat a lot of lamb, goat and mutton, in the south of Italy, white meats like lamb, kid, rabbit and pork and, in some regions, horse. In the Arabic speaking countries the most famous tagine is made of lamb, and kebabs are usually lamb or mutton.
In the South of Italy beef was eaten on Sunday, generally in the form of ragù, that is a tomato sauce in which the meat is slowly cooked over a period of two days. On a Sunday the meat ragù was eaten as a pasta sauce: basically a complete one course meal. The famous *"pasta with meatballs",* so common in traditional Italo-American restaurants, is simply an "exported" variation of this southern Italian family custom.
Meat was therefore consumed occasionally: a choice forced by poverty. Its proteins were substituted by legumes. This necessity became a declared virtue after scientists started to study the effects on our health of this dietary regime.

The first to discover the benefits of this diet was Prof. Ancel Keys of the University of Minnesota, who coined the term Mediterranean Diet. After spending a period of time in the 1950s in southern Italy, in Cilento, and observing the very low incidence of cardiovascular illnesses in the inhabitants, Ancel Keys and his team carried out a study comparing the eating habits of the populations of the United States, Japan, Italy, Greece, Yugoslavia, Holland and Finland (*The Seven Countries Study*). From the study it emerged that the incidence of death from cardiovascular diseases was much lower among the populations living around the Mediterranean. In fact, the higher the consumption of animal fats, the higher the frequency of cardiovascular diseases. The higher level of mortality of the other populations included in the research was attributed to the diet which included a large proportion of saturated fats such as lard, butter and red meat.

This is why the famous pyramid of the Mediterranean diet (see page 189) places red meat at the top: this means that it should not be eaten more than once a week. For the same reason the pyramid recommends olive oil as a substitute for lard and butter.

This does not mean that we should demonize red meat but we should be aware of the basic principles and adopt a diet that is leaner and where meat is present in its less fatty forms.

Meat carpaccio

Extra virgin olive oil combines well with meat, especially raw meat, both beef and veal; it is at its best with so-called **carpaccio.** Carpaccio was invented by Arrigo Cipriani, the owner of Harry's Bar in Venice. Its name comes from Vittore Carpaccio, a famous Renaissance Venetian painter. The dish was created in 1950, the year of the great Carpaccio exhibition in Venice and was inspired by a noblewoman, a regular customer at Harry's Bar, who had been forbidden to eat cooked meat by her doctor. There is an infinite number of versions of carpaccio, maybe one for every restaurant in the world. Carpaccio is generally prepared from fillet, or better still, sirloin steak. Before slicing, the meat can be frozen in order to obtain thinner slices. You can, however, ask the butcher to cut the fresh meat thinly with the slicer, but in this case it must be used within two hours.

Ingredients

- Veal
- Extra virgin olive oil
- Ground pepper

Preparation

Clean the meat removing all the fat, the nerves and the cartilage, to obtain a small cylinder of tender meat to keep in the fridge.
When it is thoroughly cold, slice it very thinly. Place the slices on a dish, lightly salt the meat and place the dish in the fridge for at least five minutes. Serve, dressing with a little extra virgin olive oil and some ground pepper.

Suggestion: delicately fruity extra virgin olive oil

Bresaola

Another common use of oil with meat is with **bresaola.**
Bresaola is a typical product of Valtellina in the North of Italy; it is seasoned salted beef. The origins of bresaola are linked to the tradition of drying meat, an ancient custom among the alpine people. The movement of people through the Alps soon led to the discovery of the excellent meats prepared in those valleys. The dry windy climate of Valtellina made it possible to use less salt in preserving and made the meat more tender and tasty.
Until the first decades of the twentieth century bresaola was known only in the North of Italy (in the area around Sondrio) but it has since been successfully sold all over Italy and also abroad.
Serve in thin slices with lemon.

Ingredients

- Bresaola from Valtellina
- Arugula
- Lemon
- Extra virgin olive oil to taste
- Black pepper to taste

Preparation

Slice the lemon and place the slices on a dish as a bed for the very thin slices of bresaola. Add the washed arugula and dress with extra virgin olive oil and black pepper.

Suggestion: Medium or intensely fruity extra virgin olive oil

In the Mediterranean extra virgin olive oil and fish have always got on very well together. This is partly because the fish from the Mediterranean is particularly tasty, compared to fish from the ocean, and does not need any elaborate dressing.
The only condiment that manages not to mask the flavor of fresh fish is the most delicate type of extra virgin olive oil.
White or blue fish, cooked or raw, is very suitable for dressing with olive oil, so this partnership has helped the international spread of olive oil to distant lands where they eat a lot of fish.
The most obvious example is Japan where there is a strong tradition of eating raw fish in the form of sushi and sashimi; the Japanese have recently discovered that extra virgin olive oil, sometimes blended with soy sauce, can happily "contaminate" fish dishes bringing out their flavor.

Octopus and potato salad

Octopus and potato salad is a very Mediterranean recipe because here octopus is caught locally. The octopus has two rows of suckers on each tentacle, which distinguishes it from the white octopus that has only one row of suckers and is generally paler.

Ingredients

- 2 pounds octopus
- 4 potatoes
- White wine vinegar
- Extra virgin olive oil
- Parsley
- Salt

Preparation

Cook the cleaned octopus in slightly salted boiling water with a drop of vinegar in it; cook it in a covered saucepan at a very low heat for half an hour or until tender. Cooking time will depend on the size of the octopus.
Leave it to cool in the water, peel it and cut it into chunks.
Peel the potatoes and cut them into balls (with a melon baller) before boiling them.
Add the octopus to the boiled potatoes, add salt to taste and dress with chopped parsley and extra virgin olive oil. Serve at room temperature.

Suggestion: delicate or medium fruity extra virgin olive oil

Salad with tuna in olive oil

Tuna is a very versatile fish, both fresh and canned. There are excellent quality tunas on sale canned either as chunks or in olive oil.
I advise using chunks and then adding extra virgin olive oil to personalize each kind of salad or dish prepared with tuna.

Ingredients

- 7 ounces tuna chunks
- 7 ounces cherry tomatoes
- 1 ounce capers
- Extra virgin olive oil
- Salt

Preparation

Drain the water from the canned tuna. Cut the cherry tomatoes in half and mix them with the tuna, adding salt, extra virgin olive oil and capers.

Suggestion: medium or intensely fruity extra virgin olive oil

Mediterranean Sashimi

This dish is simply fish "carpaccio". I have called it "sashimi" in tribute to Japanese cuisine that has introduced the world to the delights of raw fish.
The fish from the Mediterranean is particularly suitable for eating raw because, thanks to the aquatic flora, it is particularly tasty.
All fish can be consumed raw as long as it is very fresh and you know how to fillet white fish and how to slice blue fish.

Ingredients

- Sword fish
- Lemon juice
- Extra virgin olive oil

Preparation

Thinly slice the sword fish (no more than 2mm), if possible using a slicer. If preferred the slices can be marinated with the lemon for a couple of hours before serving. Dress with extra virgin olive oil.

Suggestion: delicately fruity extra virgin olive oil

...with pasta

Pasta is the most recognized symbol in the world of "eating Italian" and, given its versatility, it has become a part of the eating habits of many countries, above all of those with large immigrant Italian communities.
We think we know everything about pasta, but sometimes we neglect some fundamental differences between various types of pasta.
First of all, in this chapter we will talk only of semolina pasta, that is pasta made from durum wheat. It is in fact durum wheat flour that allows our pasta to be cooked "al dente", which is not possible with soft wheat flour.
Durum wheat pasta can be fresh or dried; the fresh variety is the "traditional" one, that is what was made at home, and therefore has as many forms in Italy as there are regional traditions. Today various forms of fresh pasta are on sale, but being perishable they have a short shelf life.
Dried pasta is the most important part of the market in terms of quantity and can again be separated into two sectors: the industrially produced type and the so-called "artisan" production. However, we have to specify that today some of the industrial pasta factories choose to produce in the traditional way.
This involves a slow drying process at a lower temperature (below 65°) just as in the old days when it was dried in the sun. Also, with the traditional process the wires (used to shape the pasta) are made of bronze instead of teflon. The bronze wires give the pasta a rougher surface so that more sauce clings to it.

In recent years pasta, like many other products based on refined flour, has been criticized by nutritionists who say that eating (and over-eating) refined carbohydrates contributes to obesity in western society. There is a scientific basis for this and in 2003 the food pyramid was slightly modified to specifically endorse wholemeal products.
Wholemeal products are defined as foods derived from cereals that have not had their original natural composition altered by refining, and therefore contain all the elements they had in their natural origin. True wholemeal flour, is therefore obtained from whole ground grains, including the husk (bran).

Not all products on sale as "wholemeal" are really so: for example they are prepared using refined flours to which bran and wheat germ are later added, which means simply adding what had been previously taken away. True wholewheat pasta is what anyone interested in better nutrition should look for.
The recipes that follow use fresh and dried traditional pasta with just raw extra virgin olive oil. They are just a few of the infinite variety of oil-pasta combinations available.
We should remember that if we have an excellent extra virgin olive oil and traditionally prepared pasta we already have the basis for a tasty nutritious dish in any part of the world.

Linguini with pesto sauce

The traditional recipe for Genoese pesto requires fresh basil and pine nuts which are crushed using a pestle and mortar with garlic, salt and oil.
However, pesto can also be prepared in other ways; here I propose a variation with arugula and almonds.

Ingredients

- 2 handfuls of arugula
- 2 cloves of garlic
- a handful of toasted almonds
- 2 teaspoons of salt
- 1/2 cup extra virgin olive oil
- Grated Parmesan cheese (to taste)
- 10 ounces of linguini pasta

Preparation

Place the arugula with the cloves of garlic, the almonds and the salt in a mixer adding the oil and the Parmesan to taste.
Cook the linguine (home made if possible) in plenty of boiling water. When the linguine are "al dente" drain them and add the pesto, garnish with toasted almonds.

Suggestion: delicate or medium fruity extra virgin olive oil

Orecchiette with broccoli rabe

This dish from Puglia is famous because of its naturalness and because of the special type of fresh pasta that is traditional to this region: orecchiette are still made by hand in all the towns in Puglia. This dish can be prepared in two different ways: sautéed in a frying pan or with raw oil.

Ingredients

- 3 1/2 pounds of broccoli rabe
- 14 ounces of fresh orecchiette
- 8 salted anchovy fillets
- 2 cloves of garlic
- Extra virgin olive oil
- Chili pepper

Preparation

Wash the broccoli rabe and remove the larger leaves. Cook them in plenty of salted boiling water until they are quite tender; remove them from the water with a slotted spoon. Cook the orecchiette in the greens water, and at the same time brown the garlic cloves with the oil in a frying pan, adding the anchovy fillets. When the orecchiette are cooked drain them and pour them into the frying pan to sauté them with the other ingredients. Add a little chili pepper to taste.
The lightest version of this dish is dressed with the broccoli rabe and raw oil, without sautéing.

Suggestion: medium or intensely fruity extra virgin olive oil

Wholewheat pasta alla crudaiola

Crudaiola is the ideal summer dish, and, because it uses raw ingredients it highlights the flavor of the individual ingredients. The pasta used can be either fresh or dried but should in any case be short.
Here we are using wholewheat sedanini produced by a traditional pasta factory in Puglia.

Ingredients

- 14 ounces of wholewheat pasta (sedanini)
- 10 ounces of cherry tomatoes
- 3 1/2 ounces of grated salty ricotta cheese
- Extra virgin olive oil
- Fresh basil

Preparation

Cut the tomatoes in half and dress them in a bowl with salt, slices of garlic, extra virgin olive oil, grated salty or marzotica ricotta cheese and basil. Cook the sedanini in plenty of salted water and when they are "al dente" drain them and pour them into the bowl mixing all the ingredients well.

Suggestion: medium or intensely fruity extra virgin olive oil

Spaghetti with Botargo

Botargo is dried fish roe. It can be the roe of tuna or mullet and is a specialty of some parts of the Mediterranean.
The best botargo comes from Sardinia and Sicily. It is also known as the "caviar of the Mediterranean". It is taken from the roe pouch, extracted whole from the female fish, which is salted, pressed and seasoned. It was the traditional meal of fishermen when they spent the whole day at sea.
Botargo has been "re-discovered" recently, and given its strong flavor, it is used either eaten by itself in slices dressed with extra virgin olive oil or grated over pasta.

Ingredients

- Mullet botargo
- Thick spaghetti
- Extra virgin olive oil

Preparation

Cook the hand-made spaghetti in plenty of salted boiling water. On a separate plate fine-grate the botargo or slice it thinly.
Drain the spaghetti when it is "al dente" and add the botargo well-mixed with extra virgin olive oil.

Suggestion: medium or intensely fruity extra virgin olive oil

...with vegetables

For combining with vegetables, extra virgin olive oil has no competition: oil is the best condiment for both raw and cooked vegetables. Of course if the vegetable has a delicate flavor it should be eaten with a delicate oil to avoid masking the flavor.
Vegetables have various origins: leaves (lettuce, beet, chicory, fennel, spinach), roots (carrots, red beets, radishes), but also fruit (peppers, eggplant, zucchini, tomatoes), or flowers (cauliflower, artichokes, broccoli). They are of fundamental importance in the Mediterranean diet.
The basics for choosing and eating the vegetables is the season and the method of cooking.
To guarantee the correct proportion our body needs of the nutritional substances in these foods it is important that the vegetables are fresh and in season. A lot of the produce we eat is labeled as "early", usually more expensive or less genuine, with additives or preservatives that can have harmful effects or create a food intolerance. Everyday we should eat at least two portions of cooked or raw vegetables, one at each of the main meals. Cooking should always be minimal in order to preserve the nutritional value and flavor of the food.
The tomato deserves special mention because it has totally overwhelmed Mediterranean cuisine, especially in Italy, and extra virgin olive oil is its perfect condiment. This combination has made possible such dishes as pizza, spaghetti with tomato sauce or simply "bread, oil and tomato".
In Europe the tomato represents an "imported product" because it origi-

nally grew in the Americas where it was not considered an edible vegetable. The Spanish brought it to Europe in the sixteenth century and for a long time it was used as an ornamental plant.
Only at the beginning of the nineteenth century did it begin to appear in the first gastronomical guides, and in particular in "Il Cuoco galante" (the Gallant Cook) by Vincenzo Corrado in Naples. It was Naples that celebrated the tomato in all the forms in which it is known internationally today.
The cooking tradition of Southern Italy is closely tied to this vegetable, and its harvest and preservation has dictated the rhythm of life not only of many farmers but of whole families who until recently would spend time preserving them for their own consumption (in the form of concentrate, sauce or peeled tomatoes).

Raw artichoke salad

Ingredients

- Tender artichokes
- Parmesan flakes
- Extra virgin olive oil
- Lemon juice
- Salt

Preparation

Take the hard outer leaves from the artichokes to leave only the tender parts. Cut them in half and then slice them thinly or cut them into small pieces. Put the cut artichokes in a bowl and sprinkle them with plenty of lemon juice. Leave them to marinate for half an hour.
Place them on a plate on a bed of green lettuce, add a little salt, a dribble of oil and sprinkle them with the Parmesan flakes.

Suggestion: delicately or medium fruity extra virgin olive oil

Boiled Lampascioni

Lampascioni are bitter tasting wild bulbs that grow on uncultivated land. They come to the surface when the land is plowed and are sold as a delicacy; they grow for 4 or 5 years before they can be harvested.
The bulbs are boiled, eaten in a sweet and sour sauce or fried. They are also preserved in vinegar or oil and served as a starter or a side dish.

Ingredients

- 1 pound of lampascioni
- Extra virgin olive oil
- Salt and pepper

Preparation

After cleaning the lampascioni, wash them repeatedly. You can make them less bitter by leaving them to soak overnight in fresh water and then rinsing them again the next day. Boil them in salted water until they are cooked and drain them.
Serve them hot, slightly squashed and dressed with oil, salt and pepper.

Suggestion: medium or intensely fruity extra virgin olive oil

Pinzimonio

This term, originating in Tuscany and then used all over Italy, indicates a dish, served at the beginning or end of the meal, of raw vegetables dipped in oil and salt.
For pinzimonio you need fresh vegetables and an excellent extra virgin olive oil; generally we use carrots, fennel, celery, cucumber and radishes.
Pinzimonio is a very old dish, already common at banquets during the renaissance when great trays overflowing with fruit and vegetables would decorate the tables, before being eaten at the end of the meal.
Obviously the role of the extra virgin olive oil is of primary importance. It is generally served at the table in small bowls with added salt and sometimes pepper. I don't advise adding vinegar as this would detract from the flavor of the oil.

Suggestion: medium or intensely fruity extra virgin olive oil

Grilled vegetables

Grilling vegetables is ideal for those who like raw vegetables and is a very simple form of cooking.

Ingredients

- Zucchini
- Yellow, green and red peppers
- Eggplants
- Red radicchio
- Large tomatoes
- White onions
- 2 cloves garlic
- Extra virgin olive oil
- Parsley
- Salt

Preparation

After carefully washing and drying all the vegetables thinly slice the zucchini lengthwise. Peel and cut the peppers into pieces and remove their seeds. Cut the tomatoes in half. Peel the onions and cut them into rings. Cut the eggplants in thin slices. Cut the whole radicchios in half lengthwise. Place the vegetables on a very hot grill and leave them to cook for 2-3 minutes on each side. Spread the vegetables on a serving plate and before serving dress with salt, oil and possibly some chopped garlic and parsley.

Suggestion: medium or intensely fruity extra virgin olive oil

...with legumes

Extra virgin olive oil with dishes based on legumes is a traditional combination in many parts of Europe and the Mediterranean.
The most common legumes: beans, chick peas, peas, lentils and fava beans, are a very common food on our tables. These, in fact, belong to the category known as "poor food" simply because the ingredients are so cheap, not because they are not tasty or nutritious. The peasant culture of Italy lived on legumes until the 1950s, mainly cooked in soups, alone or all together, because they are full of protein and therefore an excellent meat substitute.
There are clear historical reasons for the constant presence of legumes in our diet. In the Middle Ages the whole of Europe risked population decline because of the high rate of mortality caused by a series of epidemics capable of wiping out whole nations. The people, above all the poor, suffered from malnutrition because they couldn't buy expensive foodstuffs like meat, one of the few foods able to supply the protein needed to build up their debilitated immune systems.
From the tenth century widespread legume cultivation helped to improve the health of the people, making them more disease resistant and allowing our continent to rapidly repopulate. From the sixteenth century onwards, with the discovery of America and the subsequent importing of agricultural products from the new continent, beans arrived. It was thanks to the men of those times that these seeds were transformed into food which quickly became available for all, due to its cheapness. Legumes are currently sold fresh, dried, frozen and canned; they usually need a lot of cooking depending on the type, and if dried they also need soaking prior to cooking. In the Mediterranean area it is common to serve legumes with cereals which offers a complete meal (cereals are nutritionally complementary to legumes).

...But the fact is, we are still here — I mean we Europeans, but also those descendants of the Pilgrim Fathers and the Spanish conquistadors — because of beans. Without beans, the European population would not have doubled within a few centuries, today we would not number in the hundreds of millions and some of us, including even readers of this article, would not exist...

Umberto Eco

How the beans saved civilization

Hummus

Hummus is one of the better known Arab dishes, typical above all of Lebanon and Syria; it is a cold cream of chick peas and is by now a classic part of Mediterranean cuisine. *Hummus* is a very old dish and is usually served as a *meze*, that is a starter, with pieces of *pita bread.* The word "hummus" in Arabic simply means chick peas. In Arab countries it is prepared with *tahini,* a cream made of sesame seeds that can be bought at specialized delicatessens but can also easily be prepared at home with toasted sesame seeds mixed in the blender with extra virgin olive oil.

Ingredients

- Dried chick peas
- Garlic
- Extra virgin olive oil
- Lemon juice
- *Tahini*
- Salt
- Paprika powder

Preparation

Soak the chick peas overnight in at least twice their volume of cold water and wait until they double in size. Drain them and place them in a saucepan in which you have fried some garlic in oil. Add water and salt and bring to the boil, cook until the chick peas are soft. Drain the chick peas and put them in a blender with some cloves of garlic, the lemon juice and the *tahini.* Serve sprinkled with a little paprika and dress with extra virgin olive oil.

Suggestion: medium fruity extra virgin olive oil

Soup with pasta, beans and olio santo

Pasta with beans is one of the most traditional dishes in Italy, and being common in many areas, there are several variations.
The recipe for pasta with beans was born in the inns of ancient Rome as a cheap dish that was tasty and nutritious. Over time pasta with beans became the dish of the peasant farmers and workers who could only eat what they produced.

Ingredients

- Cannellini beans
- Short pasta
- Tomato puree
- Garlic, celery, carrot, sage, bay leaf
- Oil flavored with chili pepper
- Salt

Preparation

Soak the beans overnight in cold water with some bicarbonate. The following day, change the water and cover the beans with water to a depth of 3 inches. Bring them to the boil over a medium heat adding a clove of garlic and the herbs and vegetables. After about an hour and a half add the salt so that the skin stays soft. Drain the beans from their cooking water and put them in a pot where you have previously prepared a sauce with oil, garlic (lightly browned) and some peeled tomatoes. Add hot water and cook the short pasta with all the other ingredients.
When the pasta is cooked serve the soup hot in bowls with "olio santo" - oil flavored with chili pepper.

Fava bean puree

Ingredients

- 1 pound of peeled dried fava beans
- 1 Potato
- 1 Onion
- Extra virgin olive oil
- Salt

Preparation

Leave the fava beans to soak overnight. The next day rinse them in running water. Place some slices of potato at the bottom of an earthenware cooking pot to stop the beans from sticking to the bottom; pour the beans into the pot with the onion and cover to a height of two inches of water above the beans. Cook for 45 minutes on a high heat and when a foam starts to appear on the surface remove it with a spoon. If necessary add more boiling water. The fava beans will turn to puree, after which turn off the heat and add salt and extra virgin olive oil, blending the puree with a hand held mixer.
Fava bean puree is generally served with boiled vegetables; it is excellent with wild chicory.

Suggestion: medium or intensely fruity extra virgin olive oil

...in frying

By frying we mean all the cooking methods at temperatures around 170°C/180°C submerging the food in animal or vegetable fat.
Frying is common throughout the world and has been known since ancient times. Already in ancient Rome sweet or savory food was fried in olive oil or lard.
Today the question of whether to fry in olive oil, and in particular extra virgin olive oil, is fiercely debated by chefs, nutritionists and gastronomes.
Opinions on taste are always very personal and consequently it is very difficult to convince someone who loves a neutral taste in frying to use extra virgin olive oil. Here I would like to look mainly at the objective properties of extra virgin olive oil for frying.
During frying it is of prime importance to keep an eye on the temperature: the frying fat should not exceed the **smoke point,** the point at which the fat starts to smoke, making it difficult to breathe and stinging the eyes. Beyond the smoke point the molecular structure changes and produces residues that are toxic to our organism (eg. *Acrolein* an extremely toxic and carcinogenic substance).
The smoke point is different for each type of fat. Extra virgin olive oils have a higher smoke point (210 – 260°C) than other oils like seed oil (110 – 160°C). Choosing the latter is merely a question of cost, not health.
The high smoke point makes extra virgin olive oil the most healthy product for frying, as long as one sticks to the fundamental rules.

1. Fry in plenty of oil;
2. Fry in fresh oil (not re-used);
3. Take the temperature to 150 –

160 degrees centigrade (home frying) without reaching the smoke point;
4. Do not put large quantities of food in the oil to avoid lowering the temperature with the result that the food will absorb too much oil.

Is it better to use extra virgin olive oil or olive oil? This depends basically on taste.

Good quality extra virgin olive oil is much more highly flavored, and during the cooking it transfers part of its flavor to the food.

Potato croquettes

Ingredients for the dough

- 2 pounds of white potatoes
- 3 1/2 ounces of Parmesan cheese
- Grated nutmeg
- Pepper
- Salt
- 2 eggs

Ingredients for the breading and frying

- Bread crumbs
- 3 eggs
- Extra virgin olive oil

Preparation

Boil the potatoes with their skins, then peel them and mash them. Put the puree in a large pot and add the eggs, the grated cheese, salt, ground pepper and the grated nutmeg. Mix all the ingredients.
Roll the mixture in the palm of your hand to make cylinders about 8 cm long and 3 cm in diameter. These will be dipped in the beaten eggs and then rolled in the breadcrumbs.
Fry the croquettes 2 or 3 at a time in a deep pan or a fryer with plenty of extra virgin olive oil until they are golden brown (2-3 minutes). The temperature of the oil must be between 140° and 180° C.
Remove the croquettes from the oil with a perforated spoon and place them on a plate with kitchen paper to absorb the excess oil. Serve hot.

Fried fish

Frying makes the fish particularly inviting. It is, however, one of the most difficult dishes to cook properly. It is not easy to obtain a perfect fry, that is golden and crisp outside, soft and well cooked inside. More often than not the outside is soft and oily or it is not well cooked.
You can avoid these problems by following some fundamental rules which apply to every type of frying. Use the right pan: thin, made of iron and without a non-stick surface. It is very important to check the temperature of the oil (only extra virgin olive oil), which should be between 140 and 180 degrees according to the size of the fish to be cooked.
The principal is that the bigger the fish, the lower should be the temperature of the oil so that it can cook well inside. If the temperature is too high the fish will cook outside while the inside remains raw.
On the other hand too low a temperature will have the opposite effect: the flour coating, instead of becoming crisp and golden will absorb too much oil and will be soft and greasy. Small fish like sardines need a higher temperature because they cook in less time.
It is also important not to put too many pieces in the oil at the same time because the temperature will quickly drop with the same result as before. With very big fish you need to cut them into fillets, while smaller ones can be cooked whole.
Fish has a very delicate flesh and should never be cooked without a coating. This can be just a coating of flour, which is also much lighter.
To stop the flour coming off the fish during frying it is important to dry the fish well before applying the flour. Once it is fried add salt and serve with fresh lemon.

Panzerotti

Ingredients

- 2.2 pounds of white flour
- 1 cube of yeast 25 gr
- 1 spoonful of salt
- 3 spoonfuls of extra virgin olive oil
- 10 ounces of chopped canned peeled tomatoes
- 4 large fresh mozzarellas
- 7 ounces of grated Parmesan cheese

Preparation

Place the flour in a circle on the work surface with a hollow in the middle, pour in the extra virgin olive oil, the salt and the yeast dissolved in two glasses of warm water. Mix the ingredients well and add the warm water to obtain a soft elastic dough. Form it into a loaf and cover it with a damp cloth and leave it to rise.

Once it has risen, take the dough, kneed it once more and break it into balls. Prepare the filling with the mozzarella cut into small pieces, the chopped tomatoes, the grated Parmesan, the salt and pepper. Drain the liquid in a strainer for at least half an hour. Take the balls of dough and with a rolling pin roll them into disks. Place the filling in one half of the disk. Fold the empty half over the full one to create a half moon. Seal the edges with of a fork. Fry them immediately in plenty of extra virgin olive oil at about 180° C turning them until they are golden. Drain them on a plate with kitchen paper.

...in desserts

The use of olive oil in preparing desserts is very common in the Mediterranean. You find it in recipes for biscuits, wafers and cakes in all the Mediterranean countries from Greece to Southern Italy, from Spain to Morocco.

Some desserts made with olive oil have become very popular, like Andalusian *"Tortas de Aceite"* that come from a centuries' old tradition and are basically biscuits made of refined flour, extra virgin olive oil, sesame seeds and anise.

All traditionally fried desserts use olive oil, for example *zeppole* and *cartellate* in Southern Italy, or *loukoumades* in Greece. Of course the oil used should have a delicate flavor to avoid changing the final flavor of the dish.

A recent development in the use of extra virgin olive oil in the preparation of desserts comes from its use as an **aroma.** In the past few years there have been successful experiments particularly in preparing desserts such as mousse and ice-cream.

Ice-cream with extra virgin olive oil is one of the best uses of oil as an aroma; it can be found in top quality restaurants and in some home-made ice cream parlors. Here we give you the version used in the *Gabrielino* ice cream parlor in Puglia. It has been christened Olivio!

Olive oil cookies

These are traditional cookies whose main ingredient is extra virgin olive oil. The oil substitutes butter and makes them more genuine and lighter. Cookies with olive oil are good for breakfast and excellent with tea.

Ingredients

- 14 ounces of white flour
- 5.3 ounces of sugar
- 2 eggs
- Cinnamon
- 1/2 cup of extra virgin olive oil
- A pinch of salt
- Toasted almonds

Preparation

Mix all the ingredients and kneed to obtain a smooth homogeneous dough. Cut the pastry into pieces and divide it into sticks. Add a couple of toasted almonds to each stick.
Cook in a hot oven at 180° C for 10 minutes.

Suggestion: delicately fruity extra virgin olive oil

Ring shaped olive oil cake

Just as with the cookies, olive oil can substitute butter in many of the traditional cakes making them lighter, as long as you use a delicate extra virgin olive oil to avoid it transferring a strong flavor.

Ingredients

- 7 ounces of white flower
- 5.2 ounces of sugar
- 2.8 ounces of extra virgin olive oil
- 3 eggs
- 1 spoonful of milk
- 1 sachet of yeast for cakes
- Grated lemon rind

Preparation

Separate the yolks from the whites. In a bowl beat the yolks with the sugar to make a thick frothy mixture. Whisk the whites and gradually mix them into the yolk-sugar mixture. Add the flour little by little and slowly pour in the olive oil. Mix the ingredients well. Finally add the lemon rind and the yeast. Grease a ring shaped pan, sprinkle flour onto it and add the mixture. Bake in the oven for 40 min. at 180°C.

Suggestion: delicately fruity extra virgin olive oil

Cappelli's olive oil cocktail

Ingredients

Simple syrup

- 1 cup sugar
- 1 cup water

Cocktail

- 3 medium basil leaves, torn
- 1 small basil leaf for garnish
- 1 1/2 ounces fresh grapefruit juice
- 1 1/2 ounces premium vodka
- 1/2 ounce extra virgin olive oil
- 1/4 ounce simple syrup

Preparation

Combine sugar and water in a small saucepan; bring to a boil over a medium high heat, stirring to dissolve sugar, about 3 minutes. Remove from heat, let cool and refrigerate in a tightly sealed jar until ready to use. Syrup keeps, covered and chilled, for 3 months.
Drop torn basil leaves into a cocktail shaker; fill shaker with ice. Add grapefruit juice, vodka, oil and simple syrup; shake vigorously at least 10 seconds. Strain into a martini glass and garnish with small basil leaf.

Suggestion: Medium fruity extra virgin olive oil

... dried tomatoes
tied with a string
and women with hearts of chicory.
Dried tomatoes and yellow dates,
and women picking olives
among the wild olive trees,
with purple mouths...
Vittorio Bodini

Vegetable preserves in olive oil

Vegetable preserves in olive oil

In ancient times man was quite rightly concerned with gathering stores and food to sustain him, that is to ensure his survival, using basic methods and instruments.

Among the techniques for preserving, keeping food in oil is typical of the areas where oil is produced, and is generally used for vegetables such as dried tomatoes, artichokes, zucchini, eggplants, asparagus, peppers etc. This type of preserving involves completely immersing the food, that has previously been partly cooked or treated with vinegar, in oil. This blocks the production of micro-organisms.
We do not, however, advise preserving at home, because while the oil protects the food from contact with the air, thus preventing the aerobic micro-organisms from developing, it does not stop the anaerobic ones (such as botulin) and as a result you need to use heat treatments such as pasteurization or sterilization.
In other words: it's better to buy vegetable preserves from a reliable producer.
However, here is an example of how to preserve dried tomatoes in extra virgin olive oil, a tradition present in many of the Southern regions where the extreme heat of the summer dries these vegetables in a relatively short time.

Dried tomatoes in olive oil

Ingredients

- Approx. 4 1/2 pounds of ripe fresh tomatoes (San Marzano or Pachino)
- 2 whole garlics
- Parsley
- Salt
- White wine vinegar
- Extra virgin olive oil

Preparation

Cut the tomatoes in half, put salt on the surfaces and lay them on a flat surface, preferably wooden. Leave them to dry in the summer sun for 7 – 10 days (depending on the weather). Bring them inside immediately if it rains. Once they are completely dry open them up and give them a light wash in white wine vinegar. Place the tomatoes in a preserving jar putting some garlic and parsley between each layer, and fill the jar to the brim with extra virgin olive oil. Check the level of the oil for a few days and when this has stabilized seal the jar and leave it in a dark dry place for about a month. This will produce 1 kg of dried tomatoes.
Research shows that drying edible plants like tomatoes significantly increases their nutritional value.

Tomatoes

When I see tomatoes ripening
I say think what you could make
a plate of pasta without tomatoes
is like a garden without flowers ...
What would the world be without Americans
I don't know if
it would be a great advantage
I know that if Columbus hadn't made that journey
the world would be without tomatoes ...

... just think of "Norma" without eggplants
fava bean puree without chicory
if there is no basil
there is no more pesto
boiled potatoes without olive oil ...

... when I see them gathering the olives
I say think how bad
our salad would be without good oil
like being together without laughter

... it's just as well there are tomatoes
I say think what it would be
a plate of pasta without tomatoes
is like a garden without flowers ...

Gino Paoli (singer-songwriter)

Aromatic olive oils are an innovation with extra virgin olive oil and are enjoying considerable success because they allow the preparation of simple quick dishes with extra flavor.
It is, however, best to specify a few fundamental differences between the oils on sale: one should choose oils that do not contain essences and have been hand produced using fresh products. The use of essences makes the flavor of the oil artificial, thus changing the taste of the food.
Essences are a complex mixture of natural extracts of plants and fruits combined with molecules with defined aromatizing properties that reproduce a very similar taste to natural foods. Reading the list of ingredients on nearly all foods you will see the word "flavoring" which means that the flavor has been artificially enhanced but the taste derives from the flavoring and not from the natural ingredients.
In the case of aromatic oils, except for those with truffle, which are obtained only with artificial flavoring, the taste can be obtained with fresh products.
For example, oils flavored with lemon can use fresh lemons instead of essences. These are crushed together with the olives to produce an excellent result because the taste of the lemon will be very delicate.
The same goes for oils flavored with herbs (basil, rosemary etc.); in the process that uses fresh products the herbs are dried and then left in an infusion in the oil in the same way in which we produce at home oil with chili pepper, known also as "olio santo".

Olio santo

In the Mediterranean tradition home made aromatic oil is the so-called "olio santo", that is oil with chili pepper which is very simple to make anywhere.

Ingredients

- 5 fresh red hot chili peppers
- Extra virgin olive oil

Preparation

Cut the top off the peppers and take out most of the seeds. Leave them to dry for 5 days in a cool dry place. When they are dry place them in a 400 ml glass jar and cover them with extra virgin olive oil. Leave it for a month before using.

Oil with chili peppers goes well with many dishes; it is customary to use it in bean soups and it goes well with all those dishes that are also good when spicy.

At that time in Malaga a real passion for olive oil awoke in me.
I used it everywhere. I would start in the morning
drowning my toasted bread in a dish with oil
in which a shoal of anchovies was swimming.
I would drink the large amount
that was left in the bowl as if it were a precious liquid.
Finally I would pour the last drops onto my head and chest.
I rubbed it into my hair which started to grow again
and became so strong that it broke my combs.

Salvator Dalì

Olive oil and beauty

Olive oil and beauty

Yesterday

Studies confirmed by archaeological finds have shown that the olive originates from Asia Minor and from there the Greek merchants took it to their home country and to the colonies of Magna Graecia and to Sicily, gradually creating an oil trade throughout the Mediterranean. As well as in cooking, the use of "liquid gold" revolutionized the world of sport and of male and female beauty. For example, olive oil was used to anoint wrestlers' bodies to stop them from being gripped by their adversary, and after the match it was removed with a special instrument called a strigil. In the Roman baths it was used for massages. Women used it against aging and applied it to face and body, rubbing in small amounts until it was totally absorbed. We also know that the Romans used olive oil in certain gynecological practices during birth. It was in the Orient, however, that olive oil was first used as a base for perfumes through the processes of pressing and enfleurage, since the ancients did not know of distilling. In particular enfleurage was carried out in *onfacio*, that is in oil from green olives, with perfumed substances and red colorants. The rose of Rhodes, the *rhodinum,* was the most valued essence in ancient times, famous for its aphrodisiac qualities. The mixture was made up mainly of unripe olive oil and rose petals, to which were added small quantities of ginger, rosewood and acorus.

Today

Even today oil is still used as one of the most efficient and natural beauty remedies:
- it is excellent for stretch marks, a daily massage with olive oil makes the tissues more elastic. It is particularly indicated for pregnant women.
- Very good for restructuring hair that has been treated and weakened. An overnight olive oil pack gives you strong shiny hair.
- Mixed with fine salt it makes a good face and body scrub (in ancient times women used it once a month).
- Patted onto the drier parts of the face with the fingertips until it has all been absorbed, it is a wonderful anti-wrinkle treatment.
- A few drops in the bath water makes your skin smooth.

In fact, olive oil is often used in cosmetics, in lotions for the body and for hair, in creams and soaps. At the Masseria San Domenico near Fasano they have even produced special amenities for their guests made from their estate's olive oil.

Shower Gel
Conditioner
Shower Gel
Body Lotion
Shampoo
...dalle olive
della Masseria
San Domenico
Conditioner
...dalle olive
della Masseria
San Domenico
Shower Gel
...dalle olive
della Masseria
San Domenico
Body Lotion
...dalle olive
della Masseria
San Domenico
Shampoo

... olive oil has few saturated fats.
The essential part of my theory
is that our food should have
a limited amount of saturated fatty acids
because they increase the cholesterol in our blood.

Ancel Keys

More...

Frequently asked questions

by Alfredo Marasciulo – Panel chef and university expert in sensorial evaluation of virgin olive oils

What is extra virgin olive oil?
According to the legal definition, extra virgin olive oil (from now on EVO) is an oil obtained from the fruit of the olive only by mechanical means or other physical processes, with a free acidity no higher than 0.8%
In other words EVO is simply "squeezed olive" with excellent chemical composition and flavor.
It is important to emphasize that only the best squeezed olives are EVO, the others are classified in descending order as virgin olive oils, or worse lampante olive oils.

What does the quality of an oil and its classification as extra virgin depend on?
The quality of an oil depends on many factors, such as the state of the olives, how ripe they are, how they are harvested, stored and processed, that all go to determine the chemical make up and flavor.
If we start from the assumption that EVO is just squeezed fruit, to get a good oil it is important that the olives are healthy and picked at the right moment.

What is the acidity of an oil?
This is a chemical and physical parameter, which cannot be detected by tasting, that indicates the "chemical state of health" of the oil and the greater or lesser degradation of the olives from which it was obtained, and therefore the quality of the EVO.
During the various processes and even before, during the growth and ripening of the olive, conditions can change the chemical composition of the oil and cause the release of fatty acids. The acidity measures the quantity of fatty acids that have been released. A lower acidity shows the oil has been produced using the correct production techniques starting from healthy olives.

What causes the peppery taste of an EVO and what does it mean?
The bitter peppery taste is given by a series of aromatic substances called polyphenols that are normally present in EVO. The polyphenols, as well as being the main cause of the flavors of an EVO, are very powerful antioxidants that reduce the oxidization of the oil and at the same time efficiently contrast the aging of human cells.
The bitter peppery taste is stronger in freshly produced oils because there are more polyphenols which gradually diminish over the months.

How long does an EVO last?
An old proverb says "old wine and new oil". To fully appreciate the flavor of an EVO it should be consumed within the year of production, but if well stored it is not rare to find an excellent EVO that is 18 months old. Of course the flavor and the bouquet diminish over time.

How do you store an EVO?
The oxidization of an EVO is accelerated by three elements: the oxygen in the air, heat and light. Bearing this in mind it is preferable to keep EVO in a cool dry place, in well sealed containers away from light and sources of heat.

Is a first pressing EVO better?
All EVOs are from the first (and only) pressing, there is no second one.
You should always remember that EVO is the squeezed juice of a fruit, the olive. Can you imagine squeezing an orange a second time after it has already been squeezed?

What does cold pressed EVO mean?
Raising the temperature during the crushing process brings more oil out of the olives (technically we say it raises the yield). This raising of the temperature, however, deprives the product of a lot of its flavors and the heat destroys the antioxidants.
In cold production (that is at temperatures lower than 27°C) the lower yield is amply compensated by a greater quality and quantity of the flavors and antioxidants. Cold pressing is therefore a necessary condition to obtain a quality EVO, on the condition that all the other correct production techniques are followed and that the olives are healthy and harvested at the right moment.

Is a filtered or unfiltered EVO better?
If it is to be consumed within a few weeks of production there is no difference. If it is to be used over a longer period it is better to filter the EVO because the particles suspended in the oil that give it a cloudy appearance could precipitate to the bottom and, since they contain water they could ferment and damage the oil.

The mediterranean diet

by Dun K. Gifford – Founder and President of Oldways Preservation Trust

For at least 10,000 years the heart of the Mediterranean Diet has been a group of traditional foods and drinks – grains, vegetables, fruits, olive oil, lean meat, fish, spices, sweets, and wine. These foods and drinks offer an extraordinarily wide range of dishes famous for their palatability – simple pita and chick pea hummus in Lebanon; lemon and lamb and yogurt in Greece; pasta with tomato sauce and a sprinkle of cheese in northern Italy; fave e cicoria in Puglia; rich seafood paella in Valencia; lamb and perfumed rice in Marrakech; and many, many more.

The Romans systemized the cultivation of olive trees during their 500 years of empire – for feeding their people and armies, for skin care, for trading, and with the pulp and pits, for feeding their animals. It was the principal dietary fat for most Romans during these centuries, as it was for other nations around the Mediterranean rim.

From these times (and no doubt earlier, too) Kings, Queens and Emperors fought each other for control of olive cultivated regions like Puglia for instance. It was a highly-prized possession because its olive oil production was so vast and its rich limestone plains so vital for their vast production of high-quality wheat. Hannibal, for example, was heading to Puglia to establish a military base when he marched his army over the Alps with his elephants; when he reached Puglia, he defeated the Roman army in a battle still analyzed for his brilliant generalship. And his army was well fed by the products of the fertile Puglia plains.

The Mediterranean Diet Pyramid

Twenty years ago I decided to establish a non profit organization that would educate Americans about healthy eating and sustainable agriculture. I wanted to challenge the alarming rise of "techno foods," and persuade consumers that the "old ways" of agriculture and food production were healthier for humans, animals, and the earth. So, naming this new organization "Oldways" was inevitable.

After considerable detailed research into the healthfulness of the peoples who ate in a variety of eating patterns – based strictly on science and palatability – I and my colleagues decided that the Mediterranean diet was an irresistible vehicle for our initial Oldways programs. Two years later, in January 1993, we convened an international group of scientists, chefs, physicians and writers for a conference to help us consolidate all the evidence we had accumulated.

At this meeting, we and the scientists introduced what we named the "Optimal Traditional Mediterranean Diet – Preliminary Concept." Despite its quite complex name, the idea behind it acknowledged in a very straightforward way two key principles. The first principle was that the quarter-century of scientific studies of the Mediterranean diet pattern provided extensive and persuasive evidence that the Mediterranean diet pattern had distinct health benefits when compared to the "American" dietary pattern. The second principle was the conclusion that the evidence for this was significant and provided the justification for a new educational program to educate Americans about the health benefits of eating in a Mediterranean pattern.

Taking into consideration the considerable variations in the dietary patterns of the peoples who live around the edge of the Mediterranean Sea, organizers and attendees drew up a document that described the common elements of the Mediterranean diet in these words:

"Plentiful amounts of fruits and vegetables; legumes and nuts; grains, breads, pasta, couscous and polenta; olives, and olive oil as the main fat; limited amounts of lean red meat; moderate amounts of dairy products such as cheese and yogurt, fish and poultry; moderate amounts of wine with meals; and sweets such as pastries and gelato a few times a week."

Coffee and tea were not included in the list, but were acknowledged as sources of pleasure, but also of calories for many drinkers.

The document was accompanied by a food and drink pyramid that quantified the relationships among this diet's food groups, and included beside it a briskly walking figure to represent the importance of physical activity, and a glass of wine to show that wine is regularly consumed in those Mediterranean countries without a religious prohibition. This graphic concept was simple and straightforward, and was accompanied by a 4,200-word technical text.

It is important to keep in mind that this pyramid was defined as a "preliminary concept to represent the Optimal Traditional Mediterranean Diet, based on the dietary traditions of Crete circa 1960, structured in light of 1993 nutrition research. The geography of the diet is closely tied to the traditional areas of olive cultivation in the Mediterranean region."

The "Mediterranean Diet Pyramid," accompanied by a lengthy nutrition science rationale supporting it, was introduced to an audience of opinion makers during a large three-day Oldways conference in January 1993, in Cambridge, Massachusetts.

It was presented by a distinguished international group of leading nutrition scientists and culinary experts, and discussed intensely and at length by a group of prominent writers, journalists, chefs, businessmen and women, physicians, university professors, public health agency officials, olive oil experts, chefs, and food and wine writers.

This meeting's impact was immediate and powerful. The USA Today newspaper reported on its front page that this Mediterranean Diet Pyramid stood as a clear challenge to the much-criticized US government's "Food Guide Pyramid." A headline in The Washington (DC) Post proclaimed that "Mediterranean Madness" had come over Americans. Chefs, and magazines for chefs, proclaimed Mediterranean foods to be the overwhelming favorite way to "eat healthy and deliciously." Television programs, newspapers and magazines rushed to explain how to cook Mediterranean foods using olive oil instead of butter. And wine publications hurried to explain wine's health benefits.

This Mediterranean Diet launched a food revolution in the US. Individuals and families learned that olive oil is a healthier fat than animal fat, that it has wonderful and distinctive tastes and flavors (just the same as wine does), and that it's delicious with salads, soups, baked goods, pasta, fish, and particularly with vegetables. There is even a small (but true) joke that sugar helps the medicine go down, but olive oil helps the vegetables go down!

From its beginnings almost 20 years ago Oldways has been the world leader in consumer education programs about the Mediterranean Diet, reporting in decades of high-level nutrition science studies that (a) it tops the list of eating patterns, and (b) leads the menus of great tastes and satisfying flavors of foods, drinks and meals. This unique combination – science and gastronomy – led to the Mediterranean Diet being acclaimed in 1993 as the world's "Gold Standard" for a healthy way to eat meals that people really enjoy.

The challenge for today and tomorrow is to expand consumer and opinion leader education programs about healthy eating and drinking. Oldways is devoted to meeting this challenge, using a foundation of the best and most up-to-date scientific studies about the nutrition benefits of the justly-famous Mediterranean Diet. Education programs of this type are more effective in attracting consumers when they are accompanied by a wide range of "how to" guides – in this case, "how to shop and cook the Mediterranean Diet way." With consumers always on the lookout for "healthy foods and drinks that taste good and don't bankrupt the family budget," the Mediterranean Diet is the hands down winner.

We have celebrated the 15th anniversary of the Mediterranean Diet pyramid in mid-November, 2008 at a large international congress in Cambridge, Massachusetts. Many of the international nutrition science leaders who were present at the first meeting in 1993 have returned, as are many of the chefs who helped launch "the Mediterranean way to cook" at that original conference.

Hundreds and hundreds of high-level studies from scientists in many specific disciplines have concluded that no other dietary pattern exceeds the Mediterranean diet for promoting long-term good health. Large American health promotion organizations are also positive about the Mediterranean Diet.

* **Heart disease**. The diet recommended for individuals who have heart disease, and for those at risk for heart disease (such as by family history) but who have not contracted it, is very close to the Mediterranean Diet.

For example, this information is posted on the website of the **American Heart Association**:

"Does a Mediterranean-style diet follow American Heart Association dietary recommendations? Mediterranean-style diets are often close to our dietary recommendations, but they don't follow them exactly. In general, the diets of Mediterranean peoples contain a relatively high percentage of calories from fat. This is thought to contribute to the increasing obesity in these countries, which is becoming a concern. More than half the fat calories in a Mediterranean diet come from monounsaturated fats (mainly from olive oil). Monounsaturated fat doesn't raise blood cholesterol levels the way saturated fat does.

***Cancer**. The diet recommended for individuals who have cancer, and for prevention for those who have not contracted it, is also quite close to the Mediterranean Diet.

For example, this information is posted

on the website of the **American Cancer Society**:
"• Eat a healthy diet, with an emphasis on plant sources.
"• Choose foods and beverages in amounts that help you achieve and maintain a healthy weight.
"• Eat five or more servings of a variety of vegetables and fruits each day.
"• Choose whole grains over processed (refined) grains and sugars.
"• Limit your consumption of processed and red meats.
"• If you drink alcoholic beverages, limit consumption."

***Diabetes**. The diet recommended for individuals who have diabetes, and for prevention for those who have not contracted it, is also quite close to the Mediterranean Diet:
For example, this information is posted on the website of the **American Diabetes Association**:
"Knowing what to eat can be confusing. Everywhere you turn, there is news about what is or isn't good for you. Some basic principles have weathered the fad diets, and have stood the test of time. Here are a few tips on making healthful food choices for you and your entire family.

"• Eat lots of vegetables and fruits. Try picking from the rainbow of colors available to maximize variety. Eat non-starchy vegetables such as spinach, carrots, broccoli or green beans with meals.
"• Choose whole grain foods over processed grain products. Try brown rice with your stir fry or whole wheat spaghetti with your favorite pasta sauce.
"• Include dried beans (like kidney or pinto beans) and lentils into your meals.
"• Include fish in your meals 2-3 times a week.
"• Choose lean meats like cuts of beef and pork that end in "loin" such as pork loin and sirloin. Remove the skin from chicken and turkey.
"• Choose non-fat dairy such as skim milk, non-fat yogurt and non-fat cheese.
"• Choose water and calorie-free "diet" drinks instead of regular soda, fruit punch, sweet tea and other sugar-sweetened drinks.
"• Choose liquid oils for cooking instead of solid fats that can be high in saturated and trans fats. Remember that fats are high in calories. If you're trying to lose weight, watch your portion sizes of added fats.
"• Cut back on high calorie snack foods and desserts like chips, cookies, cakes, and full-fat ice cream.
"• Eating too much of even healthful foods can lead to weight gain. Watch your portion sizes."

Looking back over these 15 years, it is clear that the widespread acceptance of the Mediterranean Diet continues to be based on two factors: first, the high-level nutrition evidence for its health promoting characteristics continues to accumulate steadily; and second, this way of eating's popularity is delicious and satisfying, whether it be as simple as a plate of pasta, or as complex as a long-simmered seafood stew.

This is an important point. It is essential to stress that authentic Mediterranean Diet dishes range all the way from very simple *pasta con salsa di pomodoro*, basil leaves and olive oil, to a very complex *stufato ai frutti di mare*. Sometimes an elaborate dish is the most satisfying, while other times a simple one is just perfect. It is this balance of simplicity and complexity that continues to attract master chefs to the foods and food combinations of Mediterranean dishes, along with the quite amazing powers of olive oil to be the perfect culinary companion for just about everything you'd want to eat.

Another key point is the well-known palatability of the Mediterranean diet.

Who can resist the great crusty loaves of Altamura, made from Puglia's superb golden wheat; steaming couscous with exotic Sicilian spices; sizzling grilled lamb dripping with a rich aromatic sauce of olive oil, fragrant herbs, and potatoes; perfect "little ears" of orecchiette pasta with a rich sauce of sun-ripened tomatoes drizzled with fruity extra virgin olive oil and topped with a shower of sheep cheese; the sizzle and aroma of a pan of mussels and rice; or a perfect summer salad with tomatoes, cucumbers, feta, and a lovely fresh olive oil?

No true Mediterranean meal is complete without a sweet, perhaps a fresh ripe juicy peach or a breathtaking strawberry gelato, with an espresso or a limoncello alongside, of course. And more often than not, a Mediterranean meal includes the pleasures of a glass or two of robust red or crisp white wine, with a bit of cheese that might be mozzarella, caciotta, burrata, giuncata, or ricotta.

But we must address the stubborn long-term trend in food service everywhere these days – in-home and out-of-home – which is *quick-quick-quick*. People's lives are busier, they are on the run; the always-on internet and reach-me-anywhere-anytime cell phones are steadily changing the pace of life for each one of us. Every kitchen seems to have a microwave; every gas station sells chips and drinks; every airport sells meals, foods and drinks; and most offices have kitchens. The strongest trend in food markets is prepared foods, which means that fewer and fewer young people are learning how to cook or being taught basic kitchen skills.

But the Mediterranean diet is certainly alive in many regions of the south of Italy as well as Greece or Spain, and of course also in a few other beautiful and popular tourist destinations. Some experts predict that this wonderful way of eating and drinking, and enjoying the pleasures of the table, will be swept into the dustbin of history by the tsunami of fast food, convenience food, and just plain running out of time on the day as the internet and cell phones and YouTube claim more and more of non-working hours each day. Comedians joke that before too many more years, everyone will eat all their meals in their cars, or standing up at counters!
Oldways and Slow Food share deep worries about these trends, and despite the fact that we direct our programs slightly differently, we have the same objectives. Rossella Speranza, the author of this book, as well as may other food professionals who have shared with Oldways wonderful experiences throughout the Mediterranean, is committed to safeguard the healthy food traditions of her native land.
So there is much work to do if we are to keep our cherished food, wine, cooking, and gastronomy skills alive. If we do, we have a much better chance for long and healthy lives than if we surrender to the insistent advertising for fast food, techno food, fake food, and artificial flavors.

The healthfulness of the traditional Mediterranean diet is supported by 50 years of high-level scientific evidence. It is a delicious way to eat, and to drink. It offers quick meals or relaxed meals. The world peoples will be healthier and happier by heeding the powerful lessons of the traditional healthy Mediterranean Diet.

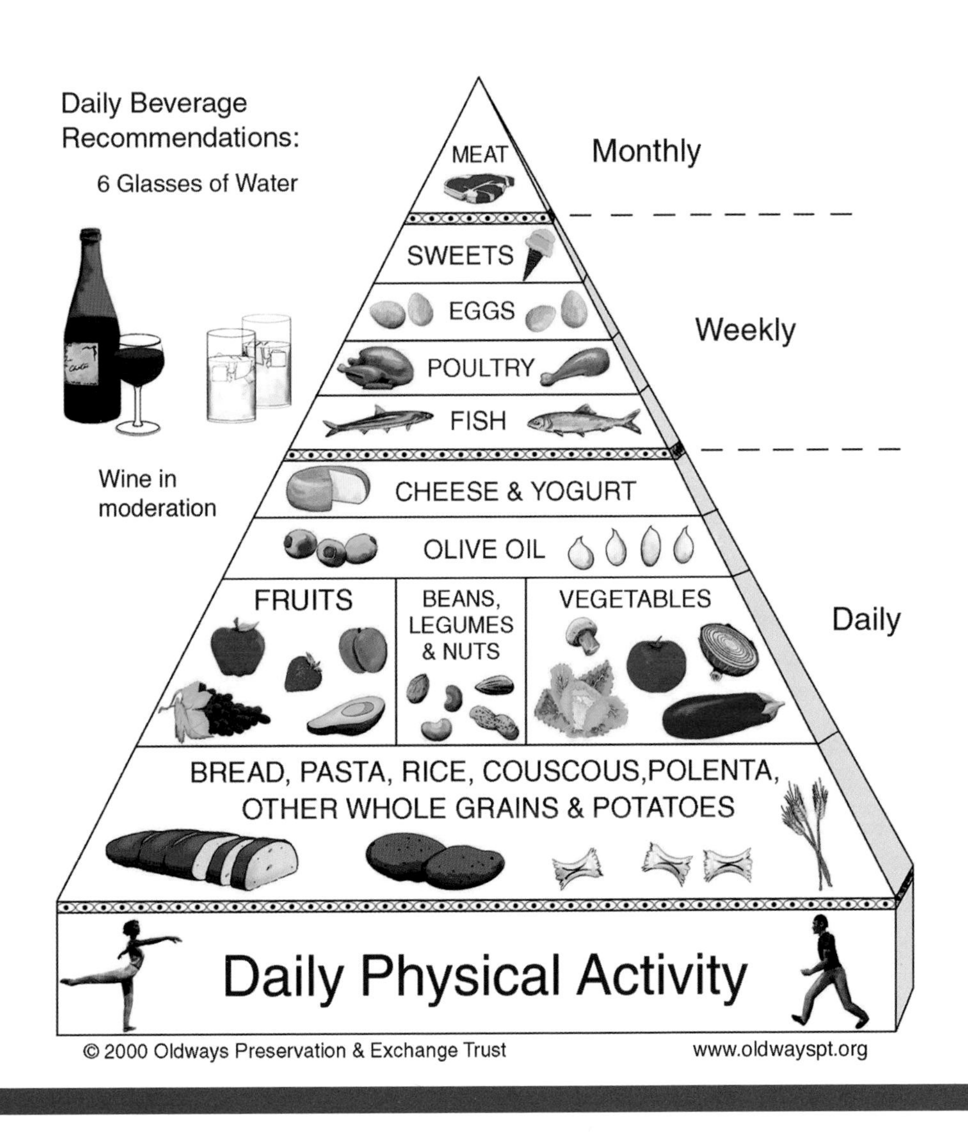
The Traditional Healthy
Mediterranean Diet Pyramid
Daily Beverage
Recommendations:
6 Glasses of Water
Wine in
moderation
MEAT
Monthly
SWEETS
EGGS
POULTRY
FISH
Weekly
CHEESE & YOGURT
OLIVE OIL
FRUITS
BEANS,
LEGUMES
& NUTS
VEGETABLES
Daily
BREAD, PASTA, RICE, COUSCOUS,POLENTA,
OTHER WHOLE GRAINS & POTATOES
Daily Physical Activity
© 2000 Oldways Preservation & Exchange Trust
www.oldwayspt.org

Profile of the Author

Rossella Speranza was born in Puglia where she studied at university and where she still has her main residence. In the 1980s she lived and studied in California where she completed an MBA in Agribusiness at Santa Clara University. During the 1990s she had a management role at the Bari Chamber of Commerce dealing with international marketing; she became increasingly interested in the food sector and the culture of the region with particular reference to the Mediterranean food tradition.

Since 2000 she has worked freelance and collaborates with foreign partners, among which is Oldways of Boston and the Culinary Institute of America in California.

She has done considerable work with the Regione Puglia and with the Ministero degli Affari Esteri for the internationalization of the Italian Mezzogiorno program.

She is coordinator for the Olivita project which aims at promoting extra virgin olive oil and its culture.

Acknowledgments

This publication is the result of a common interest in the world of oil and derives from a strong sense of belonging to a place, Puglia, permeated with this culture. I wish to thank my friends and those professional people who love this land and without whom this book would not have been possible.

First of all **Fiorella Congedo** who suggested working on the book, allowing me, through a similarity of outlook, to marry "past and future"; **Sergio** and **Marisa Melpignano,** owners of the **Masseria Cimino di Savelletri di Fasano** (San Domenico group) who, together with **Annamaria Lisi**, made me welcome in this enchanting corner of Puglia and who helped in the creation of the book; **Alfredo Marasciulo** a real professional who helped me with the technical aspects giving me some of his know-how as a passionate expert on extra virgin oil; **Pino Brescia** who, with his irrepressible creativity, manages to return to places without changing their Mediterranean charm and **Giuseppe Armenise** wizard of flower arranging, both of Botlea, Bari; chef at the Masseria San Domenico and Masseria Cimino's staff who have understood the importance of creating simple dishes with high quality ingredients, and of course, the photographers **Walter** and **Laura Leonardi** who came with us through the sun drenched countryside of Puglia.

Paul Cappelli for his olive oil cocktail.

Special thanks to **Massari family** and **Veronesi family** for the photos in their masserias.

Last, but not least, **my mother** who contributed to the organization at the most critical times.

Sources

Vittorio Bodini – Apulian poet (1914-1970)
Peaces from da "Tobacco leaves" (1945-47) e "Unpublished" (1954)

Salvator Dalì – Spanish artist (1904-1989)
Passage from "My secret life" (1941)

Norman Douglas – British writer (1868-1952)
Quote from "South wind" (1917)

Umberto Eco – Italian semiologist
Quote from "How the bean saved civilization" New York Times (1999)

Pablo Neruda – Chilean poet (1904-1973)
Full text of the "Ode to oil" from "Elemental Odes" (1954)

Gino Paoli – Italian singer-songwriter
CD "Pomodori" (1999)

Antonia Trichopoulou – Director WHO Center for Nutrition University of Athens Medical School
Quote from XV Anniversary of the Mediterranean Diet – Boston Nov. 16 -2008)

Ancel Keys – Nutrition scientist - University of Minnesota USA (1904-2004)
Passage from "The Seven Countries Study" (1980)